Day Walks Cornwall

20 coastal &
moorland routes

Vertebrate Publishing, Sheffield
www.v-publishing.co.uk

Day Walks in Cornwall

20 coastal & moorland routes

Jen & Sim Benson

Day Walks in Cornwall

20 coastal &
moorland routes

VP First published in 2019 by Vertebrate Publishing.

Vertebrate Publishing, Omega Court, 352 Cemetery Road, Sheffield S11 8FT, United Kingdom.
www.v-publishing.co.uk

A CIP catalogue record for this book is available from the British Library.

ISBN 978-1-911342-86-1

Front cover: Zennor (route 4).
Back cover: Porthcurno and the Logan Rock (near route 3).
All photography by Jen and Sim Benson unless otherwise credited.

All maps reproduced by permission of Ordnance Survey on behalf of The Controller of Her Majesty's Stationery Office. © Crown Copyright. 100025218.

Design and production by Nathan Ryder.
Printed and bound in Europe by Pulsio.
Vertebrate Publishing is committed to printing on paper from sustainable sources.

MIX
Paper from
responsible sources
FSC® C128169
www.fsc.org

Contents

* Shortcut available

Introduction

The county of Cornwall lies on a narrow peninsula that reaches out into the Atlantic from the far south-west of England. It is a place that's as much about the sea as the land, with high coastal cliffs and sandy beaches set against the ever-changing backdrop of the waves. In fact, there aren't that many places in Cornwall where you can't see the sea – or at least feel its presence in the salt-scented, wooded creeks that rise and fall with the tide. Inland, a spine of high, barren ground and granite extrusions gives way to lush, fertile land as it approaches the coast. To the east, the remote wilds of Bodmin Moor have been the foundations of many a story from the infamous Beast of Bodmin to Daphne du Maurier's *Jamaica Inn.*

Cornwall takes its name from the Brythonic tribe, the Cornovii, meaning 'peninsula people', and wall, from the Old English word for 'foreigner'. The Cornish word for Cornwall, Kernow, derives from a similar background. Home to just half a million people, Cornwall receives about five million visitors each year, mostly from other parts of Britain.

The county's opposing coasts each have their own character that sets the scene for the walks there. The north has a wilder feel with its wave-washed granite cliffs and gaping zawns – the local term for the deep, narrow, steep-sided sea inlets cut by erosion into the cliffs – while the south features a number of natural harbours and inlets, pretty fishing villages and the peninsulas at Roseland and Lizard. Both coasts are dotted with beaches, many of outstanding quality, and it's these that draw surfers, swimmers and sunbathers in their masses over the summer months. Happily, thanks to its mild climate, Cornwall is great to explore year-round and is, in many ways, even better out of season. The beaches are empty and atmospheric in winter, edged by a sea that alternates between calm, clear aquamarine and adrenaline-inducing foaming rollers as granite-grey as the local rocks.

Cornwall's sole border is with Devon in the east of the county, where the River Tamar forms a natural divide. Aside from this the county is entirely edged by the South West Coast Path, an incredible section of its 630-mile journey from Poole in Dorset to Minehead in Somerset. Much of Cornwall's best walking is to be found along the coast path, and the challenge to take on the full distance must be on every long-distance walker's bucket list.

Twenty-eight miles off Land's End, the Isles of Scilly is an archipelago of 140 or so islands, five of which are inhabited. Scilly is a wonderful walking destination with few cars and an abundance of wildlife, history and culture. Circumnavigating the islands provides some of the best routes, with surprising variety packed into relatively short distances, and regular ferries between the islands mean you can link up two or more for a longer walk. The beaches on Scilly are worth a particular mention: perfect crescents of pristine, pale sand edged by amazingly blue seas. The view from the air is one of the main reasons to fly to the islands (there are regular departures from the mainland by plane or helicopter) although there's also a certain charm about arriving into the port at St Mary's on the ferry, the *Scillonian III*.

Jen & Sim Benson

Acknowledgements

Thank you to E & H.

About the walks

The walks described in this book are between 7.2 and 13.7 miles (11.6 and 22.1 kilometres) in length and will take around four to eight hours to complete at a leisurely pace. With the exception of those on Bodmin Moor, all of the walks take in at least some of the coast path. On account of Cornwall's long, narrow dimensions it's almost impossible to create longer walks that are entirely inland. And it would be a pointless exercise anyway as the coast is so diverse in its scenery, terrain, flora, fauna and points of interest that it never feels like 'just another section of the coast path'.

For the most part the walks follow clear tracks and paths, waymarked routes and quiet country lanes with straightforward route finding and navigation. Some of the higher, more remote areas however, such as Bodmin Moor, can be tricky to navigate in poor visibility. While we have aimed to describe the routes in sufficient detail to follow easily when landmarks are visible, we would strongly recommend prior studying of the route and navigational skills and equipment appropriate to the route and conditions.

Walk times

Walk times should allow you to complete the walk at a pace that's comfortable for most regular walkers, allowing you time to enjoy the views and the occasional photo stop. Bear in mind that in the event of bad weather, getting lost, or ending up walking in the dark, these times can be extended considerably.

Navigation

Our aim is that the maps and directions in this book provide sufficient information to allow you to complete each walk. In case you need to change your plans along the way, however, it's always worth carrying a compass and the relevant map(s) and learning the skills to use them. The routes in this book are covered by the following maps in the Ordnance Survey 1:25,000 Explorer series:

101 Isles of Scilly
102 Land's End
103 The Lizard
104 Redruth & St Agnes
105 Falmouth & Mevagissey
106 Newquay & Padstow
107 St Austell & Liskeard
108 Lower Tamar Valley & Plymouth
109 Bodmin Moor
111 Bude, Boscastle & Tintagel
126 Clovelly & Hartland

The majority but not all of the coastal routes are also covered by the two 1:40,000 Harvey National Trail series maps below:

National Trail South West Coast Path 1
National Trail South West Coast Path 2

GPS

A GPS device can be a useful backup and great for checking route data. Take spare batteries and never rely on one as your sole method of navigation.

Mobile phones

A mobile phone is well worth taking in case you – or anyone else you meet on your walk – needs emergency assistance. Conserve battery life as much as possible or take a spare 'emergencies only' phone if you like to post live updates as you go.

Footpaths and rights of way

All of the routes in this book follow rights of way, permissive paths or cross open access land.

Comfort

Well-fitting boots or approach shoes with good grip protect you and your feet as you walk. Waterproof footwear is a good idea in wet conditions. A lightweight waterproof will pack easily into a rucksack and provide warmth and protection should you need it. In very poor weather take enough clothing with you that, should you need to stop, you can still keep warm. Spare clothing, food and drink will all help to make your walk enjoyable.

Safety

For the most part, the Cornish climate makes for pleasant walking conditions year-round. However, some exposed areas such as coastal headlands and moorland can experience very challenging conditions. Unusually, much of the county saw heavy snowfall in early 2018, so it's worth checking the forecast before you set out, and planning – or postponing – accordingly. Take care with high winds, big tides and cliff erosion in coastal areas; some sections of the coast path have been rerouted inland where their original course has been claimed by the sea. It's always worth carrying basic emergency items: survival blanket, whistle, first aid kit, torch and mobile phone.

Rescue

In case of an emergency dial **999** and ask for **Police** and then **Search and Rescue**. If you need the Coastguard, dial **999** or **112** and ask for the **Coastguard**. Where possible give a six-figure grid reference of your location or that of your casualty. If you don't have mobile reception try to attract the attention of others nearby. The standard distress signal is six short blasts on a whistle every minute.

Emergency rescue by SMS text

In the UK you can also contact the emergency services by SMS text – useful if you have low battery or intermittent signal. You need to register your phone first by texting **'register'** to **999** and then following the instructions in the reply. **Do it now** – it could save yours or someone else's life. **www.emergencysms.org.uk**

The Countryside Code

Respect other people
Please respect the local community and other people using the outdoors. Remember your actions can affect people's lives and livelihoods.

Consider the local community and other people enjoying the outdoors
» Respect the needs of local people and visitors alike – for example, don't block gateways, driveways or other paths with your vehicle.
» When riding a bike or driving a vehicle, slow down or stop for horses, walkers and farm animals and give them plenty of room. By law, cyclists must give way to walkers and horse riders on bridleways.
» Co-operate with people at work in the countryside. For example, keep out of the way when farm animals are being gathered or moved and follow directions from the farmer.
» Busy traffic on small country roads can be unpleasant and dangerous to local people, visitors and wildlife – so slow down and, where possible, leave your vehicle at home, consider sharing lifts and use alternatives such as public transport or cycling. For public transport information, phone Traveline on 0871 200 22 33 or visit **www.traveline.info**

Leave gates and property as you find them and follow paths unless wider access is available
» A farmer will normally close gates to keep farm animals in, but may sometimes leave them open so the animals can reach food and water. Leave gates as you find them or follow instructions on signs. When in a group, make sure the last person knows how to leave the gates.
» Follow paths unless wider access is available, such as on open country or registered common land (known as 'open access' land).
» If you think a sign is illegal or misleading such as a *Private – No Entry* sign on a public path, contact the local authority.
» Leave machinery and farm animals alone – don't interfere with animals even if you think they're in distress. Try to alert the farmer instead.
» Use gates, stiles or gaps in field boundaries if you can – climbing over walls, hedges and fences can damage them and increase the risk of farm animals escaping.
» Our heritage matters to all of us – be careful not to disturb ruins and historic sites.

Protect the natural environment

We all have a responsibility to protect the countryside now and for future genera-
tions, so make sure you don't harm animals, birds, plants or trees and try to leave no
trace of your visit. When out with your dog make sure it is not a danger or nuisance
to farm animals, horses, wildlife or other people.

Leave no trace of your visit and take your litter home

» Protecting the natural environment means taking special care not to damage, destroy
  or remove features such as rocks, plants and trees. They provide homes and food
  for wildlife, and add to everybody's enjoyment of the countryside.

» Litter and leftover food doesn't just spoil the beauty of the countryside, it can
  be dangerous to wildlife and farm animals – so take your litter home with you.
  Dropping litter and dumping rubbish are criminal offences.

» Fires can be as devastating to wildlife and habitats as they are to people and property
  – so be careful with naked flames and cigarettes at any time of the year. Sometimes,
  controlled fires are used to manage vegetation, particularly on heaths and moors
  between 1 October and 15 April, but if a fire appears to be unattended then report
  it by calling **999**.

Keep dogs under effective control

When you take your dog into the outdoors, always ensure it does not disturb wildlife, farm
animals, horses or other people by keeping it under effective control. This means that you:

» keep your dog on a lead, or
» keep it in sight at all times, be aware of what it's doing and be confident it will return
  to you promptly on command
» ensure it does not stray off the path or area where you have a right of access

Special dog rules may apply in particular situations, so always look out for local signs –
for example:

» dogs may be banned from certain areas that people use, or there may be restrictions,
  byelaws or control orders limiting where they can go
» the access rights that normally apply to open country and registered common land
  (known as 'open access' land) require dogs to be kept on a short lead between 1 March
  and 31 July, to help protect ground-nesting birds, and all year round near farm animals

» at the coast, there may also be some local restrictions to require dogs to be kept on a short lead during the bird breeding season, and to prevent disturbance to flocks of resting and feeding birds during other times of year

It's always good practice (and a legal requirement on 'open access' land) to keep your dog on a lead around farm animals and horses, for your own safety and for the welfare of the animals. A farmer may shoot a dog which is attacking or chasing farm animals without being liable to compensate the dog's owner.

However, if cattle or horses chase you and your dog, it is safer to let your dog off the lead – don't risk getting hurt by trying to protect it. Your dog will be much safer if you let it run away from a farm animal in these circumstances and so will you.

Everyone knows how unpleasant dog mess is and it can cause infections, so always clean up after your dog and get rid of the mess responsibly – 'bag it and bin it'. Make sure your dog is wormed regularly to protect it, other animals and people.

Enjoy the outdoors

Even when going out locally, it's best to get the latest information about where and when you can go. For example, your rights to go on to some areas of open access land and coastal land may be restricted in particular places at particular times. Find out as much as you can about where you are going, plan ahead and follow advice and local signs.

Plan ahead and be prepared

You'll get more from your visit if you refer to up-to-date maps or guidebooks and websites before you go. Visit **www.gov.uk/natural-england** or contact local information centres or libraries for a list of outdoor recreation groups offering advice on specialist activities.

You're responsible for your own safety and for others in your care – especially children – so be prepared for natural hazards, changes in weather and other events. Wild animals, farm animals and horses can behave unpredictably if you get too close, especially if they're with their young – so give them plenty of space.

Check weather forecasts before you leave. Conditions can change rapidly especially on mountains and along the coast, so don't be afraid to turn back. When visiting the coast check for tide times on **www.ukho.gov.uk/easytide** – don't risk getting cut off by rising tides and take care on slippery rocks and seaweed.

Part of the appeal of the countryside is that you can get away from it all. You may not see anyone for hours, and there are many places without clear mobile phone signals, so let someone else know where you're going and when you expect to return.

Follow advice and local signs

England has about 190,000 kilometres (118,000 miles) of public rights of way, providing many opportunities to enjoy the natural environment. Get to know the signs and symbols used in the countryside to show paths and open countryside.

How to use this book

This book should provide you with all of the information that you need for an enjoyable, trouble-free and successful walk. The following tips should also be of help:

1. We strongly recommend that you invest in the maps listed above on page ix. These are essential even if you are familiar with the area – you may need to cut short the walk or take an alternative route.
2. Choose your route. Consider the time you have available and the abilities/level of experience of all of members your party – then read the Safety section of this guide.
3. We recommend that you study the route description carefully before setting off. Cross-reference this with your map so that you've got a good sense of general orientation in case you need an alternative route. Make sure that you are familiar with the symbols used on the maps.
4. Get outdoors and enjoy walking!

Maps, descriptions, distances

While every effort has been made to maintain accuracy within the maps and descriptions in this guide, we have had to process a vast amount of information and we are unable to guarantee that every single detail is correct. Please exercise caution if a direction appears at odds with the route on the map. If in doubt, a comparison between the route, the description and a quick cross-reference with your map (along with a bit of common sense) should help ensure that you're on the right track.

Note that distances have been measured off the map, and map distances rarely coincide 100% with distances on the ground. Please treat stated distances as a guideline only. Ordnance Survey maps are the most commonly used, are easy to read and many people are happy using them. If you're not familiar with OS maps and are unsure of what the symbols mean, you can download a free OS 1:25,000 map legend from **www.ordnancesurvey.co.uk**

Here are a few of the symbols and abbreviations we use on the maps and in our directions:

ROUTE STARTING POINT　　　　**2** **ROUTE MARKER**　　　　**OR** **OPTIONAL ROUTE**

SHORTCUT　　　　**DIRECTIONAL ARROW**

52 **ADDITIONAL GRID LINE NUMBER TO AID NAVIGATION**

(P)BW = (Public) Bridleway　　**(P)FP** = (Public) Footpath　　**GR** = Grid reference
LHS/LH = Left-hand side/Left-hand　　**RHS/RH** = Right-hand side/Right-hand　　**(!)** = Caution

Km/mile conversion chart

METRIC TO IMPERIAL

1 kilometre [km]	1000 m	0.6214 mile
1 metre [m]	100 cm	1.0936 yd
1 centimetre [cm]	10 mm	0.3937 in
1 millimetre [mm]		0.03937 in

IMPERIAL TO METRIC

1 mile	1760 yd	1.6093 km
1 yard [yd]	3 ft	0.9144 m
1 foot [ft]	12 in	0.3048 m
1 inch [in]		2.54 cm

ROCKY COAST NEAR GWENNAP HEAD, SOUTH-WEST CORNWALL

Day Walks in Cornwall

Area Map & Route Finder

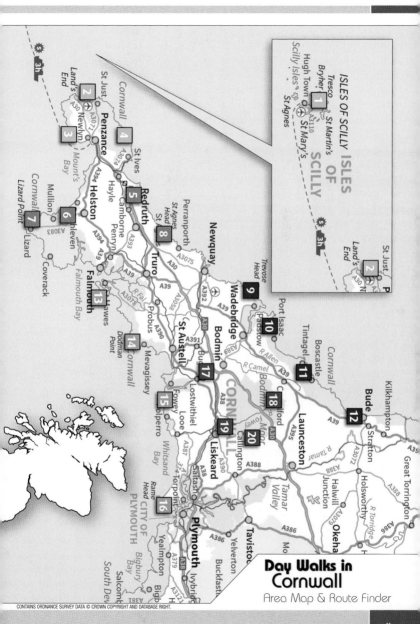

Day Walks in Cornwall

Area Map & Route Finder

CONTAINS ORDNANCE SURVEY DATA © CROWN COPYRIGHT AND DATABASE RIGHT.

WATERGATE BAY

SECTION 1

West Cornwall & the Isles of Scilly

West Cornwall, known locally as Penwith, covers mainland England's westernmost point, including Land's End. Surrounded on three sides by the sea, the coast here is dotted with stunning sandy beaches and pretty settlements hidden between majestic granite cliffs. Inland, the wild heathland is rich with remnants from millennia of human history, from stone circles to disused tin mines. The Cornwall and West Devon Mining Landscape is a UNESCO World Heritage Site and, until the last mine closed in 1998, tin (Cornish 'sten') mining had been an integral part of Cornish life for some 4,000 years.

Twenty-eight miles off mainland Cornwall, the Isles of Scilly are a fascinating place to visit. Of the 140 or so islands only five are inhabited, but there is plenty to discover from seals and puffins to exotic gardens and ancient ruins.

ZENNOR HEAD (ROUTE 4)

01 **Around Bryher & Tresco**

17.2km/10.7miles

Discover caves, coves and castles on a circumnavigation of two of the five inhabited islands in the Scilly archipelago.

Bar Quay » New Grimsby » Gimble Point » Gimble Porth » Old Grimsby » Carn Near » New Grimsby » Bar Quay » The Town » Rushy Bay » Gweal Hill » Shipman Head » Fraggle Rock pub » Bar Quay

Start

Bar Quay on Bryher unless the ferry is departing from Church Quay (information boards on the island will tell you).
GR: SV 882152.

The Walk

The best way by far to explore the Isles of Scilly is on foot, with each of the islands easily circumnavigable in a day; the largest, St Mary's, is only ten miles around. The history and wildlife on Scilly deserves a slow pace to appreciate fully – look out for rare plants, red squirrels, seals, puffins and many other sea birds. The islands are home to an amazing 239 scheduled monuments, a greater density of historical sites than anywhere else in the British Isles. The smaller islands can be linked together by boat, with regular passenger ferries serving all of the islands.

The neighbouring islands of Tresco and Bryher lie a short distance apart across a sand bar that is usually submerged under several metres of water. During a spring tide, however, it is possible to walk between the islands and three times a year there's a pop-up festival on the sand bar with food, drink and live music.

A joint circumnavigation of the two islands makes for a great day's walking, showcasing the wonderful diversity of the landscape and culture of these two distinctly different places.

Our walk begins and ends on Bryher, the smallest of the inhabited islands at just one and a half miles long by half a mile wide. Catching the first boat across to Tresco we follow the coast path around to the 17th-century Cromwell's Castle, constructed by Sir Robert Blake to defend New Grimsby Harbour during the English Civil War. Continuing around the island we visit Piper's Hole, a deep, rocky sea cave that was once mined for tin, and Gimble Porth where you might spot the local Atlantic grey seals. Returning to Bryher we explore this tiny, wild island taking in the beautiful beaches at Popplestones and Rushy Bay and the rugged outcrops in the deserted north.

AROUND BRYHER & TRESCO

DISTANCE: 17.2KM/10.7MILES » **TOTAL ASCENT**: 346M/1,194FT » **START GR**: SV 882152 » **TIME**: ALLOW 5 HOURS **SATNAV**: TR23 0PR » **MAP**: OS EXPLORER 101, ISLES OF SCILLY, 1:25,000 » **REFRESHMENTS**: RUIN BEACH CAFE, OLD GRIMSBY, TRESCO » **NAVIGATION**: EASY, PREDOMINANTLY FOLLOWING COASTAL PATHS.

Directions – Around Bryher & Tresco

➎ Take the first boat from Bryher to Tresco arriving at New Grimsby Quay. **Turn left** past the quay buildings and head north-west on to the coast path to reach Cromwell's Castle after 750m. Once you've explored the castle follow the path inland and uphill to the remains of King Charles's Castle.

2 Leave the castle heading north-west over moorland and back down to the coast at Kettle Point. Follow the coast path around the northern end of Tresco passing above the sea cave known as Piper's Hole and turning southwards to reach Gimble Porth beach. Follow the path along the edge of this and then over a small hill where you join the buildings on the edge of Old Grimsby. **Trend left** down towards the sea to the Ruin Beach Cafe.

CROMWELL'S CASTLE, TRESCO

01 AROUND BRYHER & TRESCO

Directions – Around Bryher & Tresco continued...

3 Continue south along the path above the beach around Old Grimsby Harbour to its southernmost point at the Blockhouse. Follow the coast path trending south along the east coast of Tresco. You can detour inland here to explore the beautiful Abbey Gardens on reaching Abbey Pool, 750m after the Blockhouse. On reaching the southern edge of the island, **turn right** and follow the path to Tresco's most southerly point at Carn Near.

4 From Carn Near, continue 1.5km along the west coast of Tresco joining surfaced paths back to New Grimsby. Take the next boat back across to Bryher.

5 Follow the quiet road from Bar Quay slightly uphill and **left** into town. Follow the road **left** past the (excellent) shop and over the hill by the fire station. Take a **sharp left** downhill past Veronica Farm with its honesty fudge shop to return to the coast at Green Bay. Follow the coast path around the southern tip of Bryher to the beach at Rushy Bay and from here another 500m to reach the rocky headland at Droppy Nose Point.

6 Follow the coast path trending north and bearing right up the west coast of Bryher around Great Porth and looping around Gweal Hill. **Keep left** at any path junctions, staying with the coast. Walk across Popplestones beach and then continue on to the wilder northern end of the island towards Shipman Head, continuing along the coast around the northernmost tip.

7 Return south on the east coast over Shipman Head Down, following the path above Hangman Island and then descending past the campsite and around the back of the Fraggle Rock pub to a track. **Turn left** then **right** on to a surfaced road past some houses and boat sheds back to Bar Quay.

CAPE CORNWALL

02 **Sennen & Cape Cornwall** 21.9km/13.6miles

A tour of the far west of Cornwall, taking in open hilltops, lush valleys and glorious coastal views.
Sennen Cove » Carn Brea » Bartinney Downs » St Just » Cape Cornwall » Sennen Cove

Start
Sennen Cove. GR: SW 355263.

The Walk
Our walk begins at Sennen Cove, a picturesque crescent of white sand and sheltered water popular with surfers, swimmers and sunbathers. The cove is edged by golden granite cliffs, home to seabirds and some excellent rock climbing. From Sennen we head for Carn Brea, a prominent hill topped with a 27-metre hexagonal granite obelisk erected in 1836 in memory of Francis Basset, Lord de Dunstanville, local philanthropist and head of an important mining family. Descending Carn Brea we head west, climbing up and over the high, open moorland of Bartinney Downs where there's a nature reserve and views over mining country to the sea. After descending into the lush greenery of the Cot Valley we reach St Just, the nearest town to Land's End and the most westerly town in mainland Britain. Once an important part of the Cornish mining industry, the town centre houses Plain-an-Gwarry, a theatre used for miracle plays in medieval times. The popular Lafrowda Festival is held here annually in mid-July.

From St Just we aim straight for the coast, rejoining the South West Coast Path (SWCP) just north of Cape Cornwall. Once an industrialised landscape but now a wild and windswept headland and part of the Cornish Mining World Heritage Site, the distinctive headland of the cape reaches out at the point where two Atlantic currents divide. Previously owned by Heinz, hence the Heinz Monument (a former mine chimney) at its summit, the cape was gifted to the National Trust in 1987. From Cape Cornwall we follow an enjoyable section of the SWCP back to the beach at Sennen.

SENNEN & CAPE CORNWALL
DISTANCE: 21.9KM/13.6MILES » **TOTAL ASCENT**: 709M/2,326FT » **START GR**: SW 355263 » **TIME**: ALLOW 6.5 HOURS
SATNAV: TR19 7DG » **MAP**: OS EXPLORER 102, LAND'S END, 1:25,000 » **REFRESHMENTS**: OLD SUCCESS INN, SENNEN
COVE » **NAVIGATION**: COAST PATH, FOOTPATH AND COUNTRY LANES – NOTHING TOO TRICKY.

02 SENNEN & CAPE CORNWALL

Directions – Sennen & Cape Cornwall

⑤ Take the footpath exiting the beach car park at its south-eastern corner and follow it uphill, keeping **left** at the first path junction and then staying on the main path to reach some houses. Follow the path between the houses and then **bear right** on the track to reach a road. Cross the road and follow the footpath across fields to another lane.

2 **Turn right** on to the lane and follow it around to the right into the centre of the hamlet of Escalls. **Turn left** on to a footpath heading north-east between some buildings and out across a field to another lane. **Turn right** on to the lane and follow it for a short section until you can **turn left**, cutting the corner to reach another lane. **Turn left** on to this briefly and then **right** over a granite stile, following a signed footpath across a field.

3 Cross the field to reach Trevedra Farm. Passing to the right of the buildings and staying on the footpath, **turn left** across a campsite, following a fence around to the right before **turning left** to pass through the next field to Tregiffian Farm. Follow the footpath around the farm's eastern boundary and then **turn right** at the next path junction heading north-east and gently downhill on a footpath across a large field towards the Nanquidno Downs. Stay on this path heading in the same direction until you cross a lane and reach the airport perimeter path. **Turn right** here and follow the perimeter path to the road at Brea Farm.

4 **Carefully** cross the road and take the footpath through the gate to the right of an area of scrubland. Head south-east across a field towards a track and some houses to the right of the hill. Follow the path past the houses and along the edge of a large field to a track junction opposite some stone hut circles. **Turn left** and follow the track for about 100m then take the **left** fork on to a footpath heading for the prominent obelisk on the top of Carn Brea.

5 Leave the summit and follow the track north-east downhill to reach a road. Cross the road and follow the track and bridleway directly opposite across Tredinney Common to St Euny's Chapel in the trees at the edge of the common 1km from the road (the nearby Carn Euny settlement is well worth a visit). **Turn left** at the path junction and follow the path north-west to the summit of Bartinney Downs.

6 Follow the path down the opposite side of the hill and cross the path junction at the edge of the fields. Follow the footpath across a field and south of Bartinney to the end of a lane and a path junction. Continue **straight ahead** (north) over the lane on a footpath along the western edge of an area of moorland and then **turn left** at the path junction following a footpath west to the road at the hamlet of Dowran. **Turn left** and follow the road to a sharp left turn. Leave the road and **turn right** here on to a track and then **left** out of the hamlet on to a footpath heading north-west along the edge of four fields. Cross a small bridge over a stream at Cot Valley to reach a road.

7 Cross the road and follow the footpath opposite across fields and moorland, crossing a stream at the edge of the first field, leading eventually to a track junction. **Turn left** here and follow the track to the B3306. **Carefully** cross this on to the opposite foot-path and climb up and over the hill, between some houses and down to the road in St Just. Follow the A3071 **left** into the centre of the village and then **turn left** on to Cape Cornwall Road. Follow this long straight road west and then around a series of bends. **Turn right** on to a signed footpath next to a house which heads down to the coast and joins the South West Coast Path.

8 **Turn left** on to the coast path and follow it to Cape Cornwall – well worth a detour and a wonderful place to watch the sun set. Continue south on the coast path, following it all the way back to Sennen.

VIEW TOWARDS SENNEN FROM CAPE CORNWALL

CARN-DU, LAMORNA

Lamorna & the Merry Maidens 13.2km/8.2miles

Glorious views accompany a fascinating mix of history and geology on this enjoyable walk from peaceful Lamorna Cove.

Lamorna Cove » Carn-du » Point Spaniard » Lamorna Valley » Merry Maidens » Boskenna Cross » St Loy's Cove » Lamorna Cove

Start

Lamorna Cove car park. GR: SW 450240.

The Walk

Lamorna Cove lies in a sheltered rocky inlet at the bottom of a steep, densely vegetated valley. To either side the South West Coast Path (SWCP) climbs steeply upwards to reach the surrounding headlands, giving the cove a secret and peaceful air. Our walk begins up the northern side of the valley, the narrow, hedge-lined path quickly giving way to airy trails high up on the cliffs, with outstanding views across to St Michael's Mount on the left and Lizard Point on the right. We continue along this spectacular stretch of the coast path to Point Spaniard, site of the landing of five Spanish galleys carrying several hundred men during the Anglo-Spanish War in 1595. Just beyond here is the fishing village of Mousehole (pronounced Mowsel), which was destroyed by the Spanish invaders but is now a very pleasant place to visit.

From Point Spaniard we head inland, climbing over high ground before descending back into the wooded valley above Lamorna. A steep climb up the opposite side of the valley brings us to the Merry Maidens, a late Stone Age/early Bronze Age (2500–1500 BC) stone circle. The 19 evenly spaced granite blocks gradually decrease in size from the south-west to the north-east, thought to mirror the phases of the moon.

From the Merry Maidens we pass Boskenna Cross, a hewn granite post that was discovered in a hedge in the 19th century and which was probably once part of a larger menhir (standing stone). The final descent takes us through woodland to St Loy's Cove in the pretty parish of St Buryan. St Loy's lies within Boscawen Site of Special Scientific Interest, a nationally important geological site for its quaternary coastal exposures. From here we return along the coast path to Lamorna.

LAMORNA & THE MERRY MAIDENS

DISTANCE: 13.2KM/8.2MILES » **TOTAL ASCENT**: 529M/1,736FT » **START GR**: SW 450240 » **TIME**: ALLOW 4 HOURS
SATNAV: TR19 6XH » **MAP**: OS EXPLORER 102, LAND'S END, 1:25,000 » **REFRESHMENTS**: THE OLD COASTGUARD, MOUSEHOLE
NAVIGATION: STRAIGHTFORWARD COAST PATH OR INLAND FOOTPATH AND LANE.

**03 LAMORNA &
THE MERRY MAIDENS**

Directions – Lamorna & the Merry Maidens

➔ Leave the car park heading east on the South West Coast Path over a small bridge in front of some houses and **bear right** up the hill to reach the headland at Carn-du. Continue for 2km along the coast path until you reach the end of a lane, a path junction and a house inland of Point Spaniard.

2 **Turn left** on to a hairpin bend, leaving the SWCP and following a footpath south-west across fields to Kemyel Drea. Join the track here and follow it in the same direction through the buildings and on until you cross a bridge through to Kemyel Crease and after another 500m to Higher Kemyel Farm. Continue on the footpath, bearing **right** after the buildings and walking through woodland to reach the road in Lamorna Valley.

3 **Turn left** on to the road and follow it down into the valley and across the stream. Take the **sharp right** and follow the road north-west to a bridleway forking **left** away from the road after 300m. Follow this uphill and curving left to the end of a minor road. Join this, **ignoring** a track to the left, and follow it to the road junction with the B3315 and various footpaths. Take the footpath to the **left** of the road and bearing slightly left at the junction, through a gate on to a footpath. Take the **right fork** in the path and follow it diagonally across two fields passing the Merry Maidens stone circle in the second field and then reaching the road.

4 **Turn left** and follow the road for 500m past several standing stones and an ancient gravesite to Boskenna Cross. **Turn left** on to a footpath here and follow the **right** fork across a field to the byway just north of Boskenna Farm. **Turn left** on to this and follow it round the edge of the farm buildings and continue generally south past St Loy Farm, into a wooded valley and downhill to rejoin the SWCP on your left at St Loy's Cove.

5 **Turn left** and follow the coast path east, back to Lamorna Cove.

ADMIRING THE VIEWS, ZENNOR HEAD

04 Zennor, Bosigran & Ding Dong Mine

22.1km/13.7miles

A dramatic section of the Penwith Heritage Coast, taking in rocky headlands and landscapes steeped in local history.

Zennor » Zennor Cliff » Gurnard's Head » Bosigran Cliff » Ding Dong Mine » Carn Galver » Treen » Trewey » Zennor

Start

Zennor village car park. GR: SW 454384.

The Walk

This walk takes in one of the most dramatic sections of the Penwith coast, stretching west from the town of St Ives with its stunning beaches, arts and culture. Our introduction to the breathtaking beauty of the area begins straight away with a loop of Zennor Head, named after local Cornish saint Senara. The land here is sectioned off using traditional granite hedges, found across much of the south-west. From Zennor we follow the South West Coast Path (SWCP) to the next prominent outcrop at Gurnard's Head, so called for its resemblance in shape to the gurnard fish. The pub here is well worth a visit and a great place to stay too. The headland was the site of an Iron Age promontory fort known as Trereen Dinas and the remains of a copper mine are still visible to the east.

From Gurnard's Head we walk on past zawns and coves and reach the top of Great Zawn, one of the deep, sheer-sided and quite terrifying chasms cut by the sea into this stretch of the coast, and alongside the crags at Bosigran, popular with climbers. The classic VDiff up Commando Ridge/ Bosigran Ridge is visible as you approach, a must-do if you're into climbing. Shortly after Bosigran we head inland, crossing open moorland and visiting the site of Ding Dong Mine, an extensive former mining area and part of the Cornwall and West Devon UNESCO World Heritage Site. Mining here, which local legend has it began over 2,000 years ago, ceased in the early 20th century.

From here we cross moorland and on to climb to the summit of Carn Galver, which offers outstanding views across ruined mines and ancient field systems to the final leg of our walk, retracing a section of our outward route along the SWCP.

ZENNOR, BOSIGRAN & DING DONG MINE

DISTANCE: 22.1KM/13.7MILES » **TOTAL ASCENT**: 724M/2,375FT » **START GR**: SW 454384 » **TIME**: ALLOW 7 HOURS **SATNAV**: TR26 3DA » **MAP**: OS EXPLORER 102, LAND'S END, 1:25,000 » **REFRESHMENTS**: THE TINNERS ARMS, ZENNOR **NAVIGATION**: SIMPLE COAST PATH AND INLAND FOOTPATHS.

04 **ZENNOR, BOSIGRAN & DING DONG MINE**

25

Directions – Zennor, Bosigran & Ding Dong Mine

⑤ From the car park next to the Tinners Arms cut through towards the church to the lane behind the pub, **turning left** on to this and following it on to a footpath and over a stile to a path junction where you join the South West Coast Path on the **right fork/ straight ahead**. Continue **straight ahead** briefly but take the **next right**, heading north-east across Zennor Head to reach the coast path above Porthzennor Cove. **Turn left** at a hairpin here and follow the coast path around Zennor Head and back to the junction where you turned right. Continue **straight on** to the granite stile where the coast path turns right.

2 Follow the coast path **right** and south-west passing Gurnard's Head, Porthmeor Cove and Bosigran Castle. Continue on the coast path above Bosigran cliffs, across a stream to a path junction just past Porthmoina Cove where the path forks left between two stone enclosures. **Turn left** here, leaving the coast path and heading south-east to reach the B3306 just south-west of Rosemergy.

3 Cross the B3306 and follow the zigzagging path up and over the hill for 1km to a path junction where you **turn left**, leaving the main path and heading east on a footpath between fields. At the next junction, where the fields on your right end, **turn right** almost back on yourself at first and follow the footpath around the edge of the field with moorland on your left. **Turn left** opposite the third field and head south-east across the moorland. Follow this path uphill to the old mining buildings at Ding Dong Mine.

4 **Turn left** on to the main track just past the buildings and follow this north for a short way before taking a **left fork** on to a smaller footpath before you reach fields. Follow this footpath north across moorland, climbing to the summit cairn (227m). Follow the ridge past standing stones and stone circles to the twin summit at the same height, then **trend left** downhill to a path junction at the corner of a wall.

5 Follow the path along the edge of the field in a north-westerly direction until an obvious path turns **right** and climbs to a rocky summit. Follow this a short way before **turning left** and following the ridge over Carn Galver and then **left** and back down to the road, arriving at a small car park next to old mine buildings.

6 Cross the road and follow the path from the right-hand edge of the car park towards the coast. **Turn right** at the T-junction and follow the edges of the fields along a footpath to the wall corner; here the path cuts across fields and through Bosigran Farm, across more fields and through some woodland, over a bridge and past Lower Porthmeor before reaching the road.

7 **Turn left** and follow the road, **turning left** at the Gurnard's Head pub and continuing on the road into Treen. At the end of the road **fork right** on to a footpath across fields until you come to a junction with the coast path. **Turn right** on to the coast path, retracing the outbound route to Zennor.

BOSIGRAN PHOTO: MARK BULLOCK

SECTION 2

Central Cornwall & the Lizard

The Lizard Peninsula boasts both mainland Britain's most southerly point and village. Unlike much of the rest of Cornwall, which lies on a vast mass of granite known as the Cornubian batholith, Lizard's rocks are rare, grey-green serpentinite. The walking here is varied and interesting, from the wooded creeks of the Helford River at the northern boundary of the peninsula, to dramatic, wave-washed Kynance Cove and fascinating Loe Pool to the west. Look out for rare Cornish choughs, members of the crow family with glossy black plumage, red legs and red beaks, recently returned to breed in the area.

Heading north, Godrevy and St Agnes are perfect for coastal walking, with sandy beaches, intriguing caves and a long mining history to discover.

05 Godrevy Point

A varied walk through an intriguing former mining valley and a dramatic stretch of the north Cornwall coast.

Godrevy car park » Red River » Tehidy Woods » South West Coast Path » Reskajeage Downs » Hell's Mouth » Navax Point » Godrevy Point » Godrevy car park

Start

Godrevy National Trust car park.
GR: SW 584422.

The Walk

National Trust-owned Godrevy is a popular spot with surfers, walkers and wildlife watchers. This wide, sandy beach lies to the east of St Ives Bay with a lighthouse-topped island at its entrance. Our walk begins at Godrevy car park, nestled in the Gwithian Towans – a long stretch of dunes along this part of the coast. From here, after a short road section, we head down to the Red River at Menadarva. Heavily industrialised during the mining period, this valley has naturally regenerated and is a peaceful, leafy place today, however at one time the water ran red with waste from the mines and there are still ochre deposits visible on the riverbed.

Our route now takes us through Tehidy Country Park, a 250-acre area of woodland that was once part of the Basset family estate but is now owned and managed by Cornwall County Council. Reaching the South West Coast Path (SWCP) at Basset's Cove we head west along the high tops of North Cliffs, backed by the heathland of Reskajeage Downs, to the dramatic rocky inlet of Hell's Mouth. In 2011, following a pre-emptive diversion of the coast path, some 100,000 tonnes of rock fell from here into the Atlantic. From Hell's Mouth we climb over The Knavocks where, from the trig point-topped summit on a clear day, you can see right across to St Michael's Mount off the south coast of Cornwall. Look out for seals at Mutton Cove and enjoy the final section as you round Godrevy Point where the views across St Ives Bay open out before you.

GODREVY POINT

DISTANCE: 17.4KM/10.8MILES » **TOTAL ASCENT**: 391M/1,283FT » **START GR**: SW 584422 » **TIME**: ALLOW 5.5 HOURS **SATNAV**: TR27 5ED » **MAP**: OS EXPLORER 102, LAND'S END, AND OS EXPLORER 104, REDRUTH & ST AGNES, 1:25,000 **REFRESHMENTS**: GODREVY CAFE AT THE START » **NAVIGATION**: STRAIGHTFORWARD; CLEAR INLAND PATHS AND SIMPLE COAST PATH NAVIGATION.

GODREVY ROCKS

GODREVY POINT

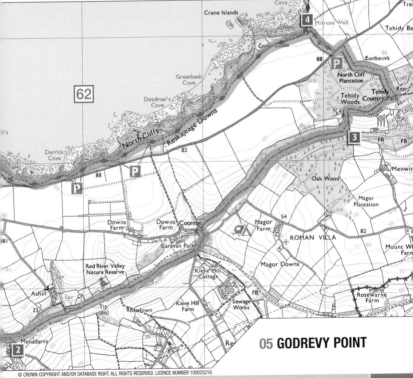

05 GODREVY POINT

Directions – Godrevy Point

5 Walk back down to the road and **turn left** following the B3301 east. Take the **first right** turn and follow a quiet, winding lane past a few houses and then uphill though a farm. At the stone cross **turn right** through a gate and follow a footpath along the edge of four fields slightly uphill and then diagonally downhill to reach a road.

2 Continue on to the road in the same direction, then after a short distance **turn right** on to a bridleway up the Red River valley. Follow this path for 1.5km, **ignoring** paths that split off to the left, until you reach a road. **Turn left** on to the road and after a short distance **turn left** over the bridge. **Turn sharp right** on to a bridleway just past a house and follow it slightly uphill in a north-easterly direction into some woodland. Follow this path for just over 1km until you reach a left fork in the path.

3 Take the **left fork** uphill, and then **left** on to the larger track, following this to the junction at the top of the hill after a short distance. **Turn right** and follow the track taking the second main **left turn** after 500m and following the path to the northern edge of Tehidy Woods; continue on the path as it trends left. Take the **right-hand path** through a stile and along the edge of a field to the road. **Turn left** on to the road and take the **first right** down a track to a car park on the South West Coast Path.

4 **Turn left** and follow the SWCP in a south-westerly direction along the top of the cliff until you reach the impressive Hell's Mouth cliffs and the cafe after about 3.5km. Continue on the SWCP as it heads north to Navax Point and then around the headland to Godrevy Point. Follow the SWCP south, joining the road and returning to the start.

PORTHLEVEN SANDS

06 **Penrose & Loe Pool**

15.9km/9.9miles

An intriguing walk on the Penrose estate taking in the peaceful Loe Pool, historical Gunwalloe and dramatic Loe Bar.

Penrose Hill car park » Porthleven Road in Helston » Degibna Wood » Carminowe Creek » Gunwalloe » Loe Bar » The Stables Cafe » Penrose Hill car park

Start

National Trust Penrose Hill car park. GR: SW 638258.

The Walk

Loe Pool is Cornwall's largest natural freshwater lake, stretching across the Penrose estate on the western edge of the Lizard Peninsula to very nearly reach the sea. A wide sand and shingle bar separates the lake from Mounts Bay making for an interesting feature around which to base a walk.

Our route begins near to Penrose House, still privately owned and lived in by the Rogers family, who gifted the wider estate to the National Trust in 1975 on the condition that it should be kept as a place of great beauty for people to enjoy without distraction. From here we follow the former carriage drive, laid in the 1840s as the main approach to the house, alongside Loe Marsh and the former silver lead mine of Wheal Pool to reach the entrance to the estate at Helston. From Helston we follow the opposite side of the lake on pleasant woodland paths before rounding the seaward end of Loe Pool at Carminowe Creek along a trail right at the water's edge. Here we leave the lake, following a bridleway to the village of Gunwalloe with its medieval church, wildlife-rich reedbeds and peaceful twin beaches. From Gunwalloe we follow the South West Coast Path (SWCP) back towards Penrose.

Our route crosses the vast sand and shingle stretch of Loe Bar, the restless sea to one side and the silver stillness of Loe Pool to the other, before climbing steeply up the cliff path on the far side of the bar. The final section of the walk follows this higher path with great views out across the lake before winding through woodland to bring us back to Penrose House, via the Stables Cafe.

PENROSE & LOE POOL

DISTANCE: 15.9KM/9.9MILES » **TOTAL ASCENT**: 441M/1,447FT » **START GR**: SW 638258 » **TIME**: ALLOW 4.5–5 HOURS **SATNAV**: TR13 0RD » **MAP**: OS EXPLORER 103, THE LIZARD, 1:25,000 » **REFRESHMENTS**: THE STABLES CAFE, PENROSE NATIONAL TRUST » **NAVIGATION**: SIMPLE LAKESIDE OR COASTAL PATH.

06 PENROSE & LOE POOL

Directions – Penrose & Loe Pool

➎ Follow the steps down from the car park to reach the estate road which heads south-east with woodland on your right to a path junction. **Turn left** here and continue over an ornamental bridge following the surfaced path towards Loe Pool. Follow this path as it curves to the left – ignoring a path branching to the right – and follow the edge of the lake through Loe Valley for about 2km to reach Porthleven Road just outside Helston.

2 **Turn right** here and cross a small footbridge into a car park. Cross the car park and **turn right** on to the path heading back south-west, initially towards the lake. **Turn right** at Lower Nansloe and follow the path to the lake's north-east corner. Continue on the lakeside path south through Degibna Wood and around Carminowe Creek keeping close to the water's edge or on the higher parallel path if flooded. Follow the northern shore of the creek around its eastern end before **turning right** and following the southern shore to the beach at Loe Bar.

3 Follow the bridleway to the left, skirting around the edge of the grass area above Loe Bar and stay left following the track slightly inland and uphill between fields and past a small National Trust car park to reach the end of a road at Chyvarloe. **Continue** in the same direction on to a footpath opposite and initially on a track, heading south-east along the edge of some fields to another road. **Turn right** on to this and follow it into Gunwalloe.

4 **Turn right** at the road junction and follow a lane past a bus stop towards the sea. After about 300m **fork left** on to a footpath heading directly to the coast and join the South West Coast Path. **Turn right** on to the coast path and follow it north-west above the beach until you reach Loe Bar where you drop down on to the beach and cross the shingle barrier between the lake and sea.

5 Follow the coast path up a steep path to gain a higher track and **turn sharply right** at a hairpin on to this, leaving the coast path. Follow this track as it traverses above the western shore of the lake, descending and then climbing again past Bar Lodge and eventually away from the lake to Penrose House and the National Trust cafe. Follow this path around to the right to join the outbound path. **Turn left** on to this and follow it back uphill. Go over the bridge, **turn right** and then **left** up the hill and steps to the start.

07 Around Lizard Point

13.5km/8.4miles

A walk around mainland Britain's most southerly point taking in the area's fascinating history, geology and wildlife.

Lizard village green » Church Cove » Bass Point » Housel Bay » Lizard Point » Kynance Cove » Lizard Downs » Lizard Village

Start
Lizard village green. GR: SW 703125.

The Walk

The Lizard Peninsula is the most southerly part of Britain's mainland, a unique place with a distinct character, partly because of its separation from the main arm of Cornwall, but also because of its unusual geology. The metamorphic rocks on which the peninsula lies are dark green in colour, veined with red and white, named serpentinite for their resemblance to snakeskin. The relentless sea has carved the coastline into an intricate maze of coves and caves, perfect for exploration on foot or by boat – the sea kayaking is also outstanding here.

Our walk begins in Lizard village, a friendly community with plenty going on all year round. From here we join the South West Coast Path (SWCP), passing the lifeboat station, home to the lifeboat *Rose*, and Bass Point lookout station. Bass Point is a fascinating place staffed by volunteers, and visitors are welcome to take in the views, learn about Guglielmo Marconi's early 20th-century experiments in transatlantic wireless communication, and chat with the watchkeeper, as long as an incident isn't ongoing.

Continuing along the coast path we round the headland at Lizard Point; the lighthouse here is one of the largest in the world and is open to the public over the summer. Keep an eye out for seals, which can often be seen hauled out on the rocks that edge the coves and beaches. Further west we explore Kynance Cove, a maze of wavewashed boulders strewn across a sandy beach. Our final section heads inland, up and over Lizard Downs, a National Nature Reserve, to return to Lizard village.

AROUND LIZARD POINT

DISTANCE: 13.5KM/8.4MILES » **TOTAL ASCENT**: 520M/1,706FT » **START GR**: SW 703125 » **TIME**: ALLOW 4.5 HOURS **SATNAV**: TR12 7NQ » **MAP**: OS EXPLORER 103, THE LIZARD, 1:25,000 » **REFRESHMENTS**: ANN'S PASTIES, BEACON TERRACE, LIZARD **NAVIGATION**: VERY SIMPLE COAST PATH AND INLAND LANES AND FOOTPATHS.

LIZARD POINT

07 **AROUND LIZARD POINT**

Directions – Around Lizard Point

5 **Turn left** (east) out of the car park in the centre of Lizard village and follow Beacon Terrace and then Church Cove Road to the coast at Church Cove. **Turn right** here on to the South West Coast Path and follow it south, passing the lifeboat station to reach Bass Point lookout station. The route now follows the signed SWCP until point 5. Continue along the clifftop path past the Housel Bay Hotel. The path drops down to the left and across a small footbridge and then continues along the cliff, passing the Lizard Lighthouse and reaches a small car park, cafe and gallery at the road.

2 Continue on the coast path, following the road uphill for a few metres before **turning left** past Polpeor Cove and around Lizard Point. Follow the coast around north and then west until you reach the viewpoint above Kynance Cove, halfway through the walk at around 7.5km.

3 At Kynance Cove, drop down to join the National Trust path to the beach. There are two paths here: stay left if the tide is low and drop straight down on to the beach, or if the tide is in stay right and follow the slightly longer path around to the beach by the old buildings.

4 Cross the stream over a bridge and continue along the coast path out along Kynance Cliff to The Rill and then north until you reach a valley with a stream, waterfalls and a path heading inland to the right.

> **OR** In winter, or if it's very wet, the following section is more stream than path. If you'd prefer to avoid wet feet we recommend returning to Kynance Cove via the SWCP and then following the road from the car park to point 6 (GR SW 69.3131) where you can rejoin the main route and follow the footpath back to the start.

5 Cross the stream and **turn right**, leaving the SWCP and following the path inland to reach a junction of paths near Jolly Town Farm. Turn on to the **right-hand** track, cross the stream and follow the track south between fields to reach a gate. **Turn left** here following the Natural England footpath south-east across Lizard Downs and crossing another stream via a bridge, then **turn right** and head uphill to the National Trust Kynance Cove car park. **Turn left** and follow a path across the moorland to reach a lane.

6 **Continue** in the same direction for a short distance, then cross the lane just after the house and use the stile to join a footpath heading south-east across a field and some scrubby moorland to some trees, **ignoring** tracks to the left and right. **Continue** in the same direction through the trees and climb up on to an interesting path that walks along the top of a wall between fields emerging behind a shed in Lizard village. **Turn left** on to the road and follow this back to the start.

SERPENTINITE ROCK, LIZARD

08 Chapel Porth & St Agnes Beacon   11.6km/7.2miles

A walk through time visiting the ruined mines of this once industrial landscape and the site of a World War II battery.

Chapel Porth » Porthtowan » Towan Cross » St Agnes Beacon » St Agnes Head » Wheal Coates Tin Mine » Chapel Porth

Start

Chapel Porth National Trust car park.
GR: SW 697494.

The Walk

Our walk begins at Chapel Porth, a sandy beach edged by high granite cliffs networked with caves that are fascinating to explore. The beach and its surrounds feel wild and untouched, however this was once a heavily industrialised tin and copper mining area and the ruins of several mine buildings still stand high on the headlands. From Chapel Porth we head steeply up and over Wheal Charlotte Moor, where disused shafts and tips remain as evidence of the area's busy past. From here we drop down to Porthtowan beach, which lies at the end of a steep-sided valley below Porthtowan village.

Our route now takes us inland to the hamlet of Towan Cross and follows two river valleys before climbing to reach the summit of St Agnes Beacon, set amidst rare and important wildlife-rich heathland that once covered a vast area of Cornwall. Descending from St Agnes Beacon we return to the South West Coast Path (SWCP) at St Agnes Head, home to a World War II battery including a hospital, Navy, Army and Air Force Institutes (NAAFI) canteen, chapel and theatre. Following the war this was converted into housing, which was finally demolished in the 1970s. The area has a long history of human habitation and Mesolithic tools and weapons have been discovered on the headland.

Walking south along the clifftops brings us to the ruins of Wheal Coates Tin Mine where production ceased in 1914. These National Trust-owned grade II listed buildings date from the 1870s and are part of the Cornwall and West Devon Mining Landscape World Heritage Site. From here we descend back to the beach at Chapel Porth and the end of our walk.

CHAPEL PORTH & ST AGNES BEACON

DISTANCE: 11.6KM/7.2MILES » **TOTAL ASCENT**: 583M/1,913FT » **START GR**: SW 697494 » **TIME**: ALLOW 4 HOURS **SATNAV**: TR5 0NR » **MAP**: OS EXPLORER 104, REDRUTH & ST AGNES, 1:25,000 » **REFRESHMENTS**: CHAPEL PORTH BEACH CAFE AT THE START » **NAVIGATION**: SIMPLE COAST PATH AND INLAND FOOTPATHS.

Directions – Chapel Porth &
St Agnes Beacon

➎ From the car park, join the South West Coast Path heading south. Initially it heads inland but then goes back on itself up Mulgram Hill, towards the sea and over Wheal Charlotte Moor. From the top of the hill continue south bearing left, following the coast path along the top of the cliff to reach the sand at Porth Towan. **Turn left** across the car park and climb the steep hill up Eastcliff. **Turn right** at the junction and follow the path, **turning left** along the houses to join Towan Road. Follow this past Towan Farm to join a larger road at Towan Cross and the Victory Inn.

2 **Turn left** on to the minor road opposite the pub and follow it downhill until you can **turn left** on a hairpin bend to follow a bridleway north-west down Chapel Combe. After about 750m, **turn right** at a fork on to a path heading north-east through some woodland and up a small stream valley until you must **turn sharp left** to stay on the footpath. Continue on this path for a short distance then **turn right** and **then left** after 300m up the edge of a field until you reach the road at Goonvrea.

3 **Turn right** on to the road and follow it, then **turn left** on to a track heading north just before the entrance to the Beacon Hotel. Follow this uphill and then **turn left** behind a house and out on to open heathland. Contour uphill, **turning right** almost back on yourself at the path junction. Take the middle track uphill where it forks into three, and follow this path uphill north-east towards St Agnes Beacon trig point and summit.

4 Continue along the ridge path and take the **sharp left turn** at a path junction near the corner of the field. Follow this path north-west downhill to reach the road at a small lay-by car park. Cross straight over the road and follow the minor road past a barn and through a set of concrete gateposts, **turning left** on to a lane that turns into a footpath following the edge of the field. At the corner of the field **turn right** at a fork, and then **trend left** across the heathland to the lane by the car park. **Turn right** on to this and follow it to the next car park.

5 **Turn left** and follow the path north towards the sea where you rejoin the SWCP. **Turn left** on to the coast path and follow it around St Agnes Head and then south. After about 1km near Tubby's Head, leave the coast path and continue on the higher, left-hand path along the edge of a field to the chimneys and beam houses of Wheal Coates Tin Mine. Explore this and then head back towards the sea, **turning left** on to the coast path and following it back to Chapel Porth.

08 CHAPEL PORTH & ST AGNES BEACON

St Agnes
Head

Crams

Carn Gowla

5 New
Downs

New Downs
Farm

South West Coast Path

Bawden
Farm

Shafts
(dis)

Mine
(dis)

Quarries
(dis)

Shafts
(dis)

69

70

Sand
Pit

Higher Bal
Farm

Mine
(dis)

Chy

Higher Bal

Quarry
(dis)

Cairn

51

Beacon Drive

St Agnes
Beacon

71

Shaft
(dis)

Shaft
(dis)

Tubby's
Head
Settlement

Mine
(dis)

Tips
(dis)

Chy

Beacon Cottage
Farm

4

192

137

Spr

Cave

Chy

50

Bolster

Dyke

Natural Arch
Cave

3

Goonvrea

Dyke

Chapel Porth

Chapel
(rems of)

PC

S

Goonvrea
Farm

Natural Arch
Cave

Mulgram
Hill

Tips
(dis)

72

Parc-nor

Wheal Charlotte
Moor
Shafts

Tips
(dis)

Shaft

Mine
(dis)

Tips
(dis)

Mean Low Water

Mean High Water

49

Mine
(dis)

Chapel Combe

Mingoose

Mingo
Far

Splatt

FING

Towan
Cross

Towan Cross
Farm

Porth Towan

Towan Farm

Shaft

Settlement

2

FB

PC

Tip
(dis)

Shafts
(dis)

08 **CHAPEL PORTH & ST AGNES BEACON**

SECTION 3

The North Coast

East of Newquay the north Cornwall coast runs along a series of bays and headlands to reach the Devon border between Bude and Hartland Point. Much of this coastline is a designated Area of Outstanding Natural Beauty and the views along this stretch of the South West Coast Path are spectacular. The intricate, wildlife-rich heritage coast around Trevose Head, just outside the bustling town and fishing port of Padstow, contrasts rugged headland with white sand beaches. The wonderfully named 'Rumps' at Pentire Point offer a great view across Lundy Bay to the Gothic tower of Doyden Castle, overlooking a deep rocky inlet at Port Quin.

WIDEMOUTH SAND FROM LOWER LONGBREAK (ROUTE 12)

TREYARNON BAY

09 Trevose Head

16km/9.9miles

A loop of the Heritage Coast around Trevose Head combining dramatic granite coastline and stunning sandy beaches.

Porthcothan » Constantine Bay » Harlyn » Cataclews Point » Trevose Head » Treyarnon Bay » Porthcothan

Start

Porthcothan beach car park.
GR: SW 858719.

The Walk

Our walk begins in the village of Porthcothan, set above its own wide, sandy bay, edged by rocky cliffs and boulders. Until January 2014, a distinctive granite archway known locally as 'The Anchor' or 'Jan Leverton's Rock' stood guarding the entrance to the bay, however it was destroyed by huge waves during fierce winter storms.

From Porthcothan we head inland, up and over the open grassy headland and through the village of Constantine Bay. The feeling of space and the views out across countryside to the coast are wonderful. At the village of Harlyn we join the South West Coast Path (SWCP), following the wide sweep of Harlyn Bay, edged by rock pools and popular with families and surfers. The two bays slightly further on, Onjohn Cove and Big Guns Cove, are slightly trickier to reach and, therefore, often quieter – the snorkelling from

these two sheltered bays is excellent too. Rounding Cataclews Point, the views open out across Polventon Bay to the prominent headland beyond. National Trust-owned Trevose Head is part of a stretch of Heritage Coast and rich in wildlife, with fulmars, razorbills, guillemots, linnets, corn buntings and skylarks to be seen on and around this dramatic promontory. The views from here are outstanding, taking in most of the north Cornwall coast from Pendeen in the south to Hartland, across the Devon border in the north – and the sunsets are second to none. Trevose is also home to a lighthouse and lifeboat station, moved here from nearby Padstow due to silting of the River Camel.

The final section of our walk rounds the white, sandy sweep of Treyarnon Bay and follows the coast path along a spectacular and intricate stretch of the coast that includes Warren Cove and Pepper Cove before descending back into Porthcothan to finish.

TREVOSE HEAD

DISTANCE: 16KM/9.9MILES » TOTAL ASCENT: 510M/1,673FT » START GR: SW 858719 » TIME: ALLOW 6 HOURS » SATNAV: PL28 8LW » MAP: OS EXPLORER 106, NEWQUAY & PADSTOW, 1:25,000 » REFRESHMENTS: STEIN'S FISH AND CHIPS, PADSTOW » NAVIGATION: SIMPLE, EITHER ON THE COAST PATH OR INLAND ON LANES AND FOOTPATHS.

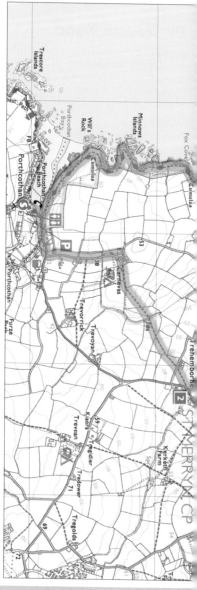

The Bull
Dinas Head
Trevose Head
Stinking Cove
Mackerel Cove
Round Hole
Cat's Cove
Chun Cove
Barras Bay
Merope Rocks
Lifeboat Station
Long Cove
Trethias Island
Treyarnon Point
Constantine Bay
Booby's Bay
Treyarnon Bay
Treyarnon
Hotel
Polventon or Mother Ivey's Bay
Trevose Farm
Mother's Cove
Toll
Constantine Bay
Trevose Golf and Country Club
St Constantine (remains of)
St Constantine
Lower Harlyn Farm
The Cellars
Harlyn
Ashlyn Downs
Harlyn Bay
Obilohn Cove
Cataclews Point
Big Guns Cove
Cataclews Point
St Cadoc's Point
Towan Farm
Towan
Higher Harlyn
Trevear
Cerny
Polmark
St Merryn
Trevofga
Quarry (disused)
St Cadoc Cottage
St Earl

323

86

87

3

4

5

09 TREVOSE HEAD

Directions – Trevose Head

From the beach or seafront car park join the B3276 and follow it north-east uphill, taking the **first left** signed to Treyarnon. Follow this road, continuing uphill to Carnevas campsite and taking the third gate on the **right** after the main entrance. Follow a footpath along the northern edge of the campsite east and then across fields trending left and **ignoring** paths on the right, then cross a footbridge and three more fields to reach a road. Cross straight over the road and follow the signed footpath opposite to rejoin the B3276 at Trehemborne.

2 **Turn left** on to the road and then **left** at the corner on to a farm lane, continuing on to the footpath at its end. Follow this north-west across fields and over a footbridge to a road at Trevear. **Turn left** on to the road and follow it north through a farm, and when it divides into three tracks take the **left fork** on to a track and path across a field to the corner of some houses. **Turn left** on to the lane and follow it with fields on your left and houses on the right to a crossroads.

3 **Turn right** opposite the Constantine Bay Stores and follow the road, **turning left** on the road in front of the Trevose Golf Club and continuing on the road past the golf course, fields and Harlyn Barton. **Turn right** on to a signed footpath through the hedge and cut across the field back to the road. **Turn right**, cross the road and immediately **turn left** on to a footpath crossing another field to a path between some houses joining a road in Harlyn. **Turn right** until you join up with the road, then **turn left** on to it. Follow this road north-east downhill to the coast.

4 **Turn left** before the bridge on to the South West Coast Path and follow it west around Harlyn Bay and out to Cataclews Point. Continue on the coast path around Polventon (or 'Mother Ivey's') Bay to Trevose Head – a short detour inland here takes you over the headland and past a memorial to two former quarry workers.

5 Continue following the SWCP south around Booby's Bay and Treyarnon Bay and then south back to Porthcothan. **Turn right** on to the road to return to the start.

PENTIREGLAZE HAVEN

10 Pentire Point

17.6km/10.9miles

A walk across fine, sandy beaches and around dramatic headlands with great views of the north Cornwall coast.

Rock ferry slip » Brea Hill » Daymer Bay » Polzeath » Pentire Point » Lundy Hole » Roserrow » St Enodoc Church » Rock ferry slip

Start

Rock ferry slip or nearby car park.
GR: SW 928757.

The Walk

The affluent village of Rock lies opposite Padstow on the north-east bank of the Camel Estuary. Set above a long, sandy beach the name Rock comes from its quarrying history, however today it is better known for being home to one of the five (at the time of writing) Michelin-starred restaurants in Cornwall. Our walk begins at the very edge of the village, heading straight out on to the grassy hillside of Brea Hill and then down to the wide sandy expanse of Daymer Bay. Skirting surfy Polzeath we reach Pentireglaze Haven, a peaceful, hidden beach at the foot of a long, grassy valley. From here we head up and around Pentire Point from where, on a clear day, there are fine views across the Camel Estuary to Stepper Point and the Trevose Lighthouse in the west and to Tintagel Castle in the east.

A prominent and wonderfully named headland, The Rumps, at the north-eastern edge of the Pentire peninsula, is the site of a late Iron Age promontory fort. Once topped by wooden palisades, the three original ramparts are still clearly visible, spanning the narrowest part of the promontory. A fascinating feature to explore, the views and feeling of remote wildness are well worth the detour; this was where poet Laurence Binyon wrote his poem *For the Fallen*, commemorated by a plaque set into the headland.

Rounding The Rumps we reach the sea cave and sheltered cove at Lundy Hole and head inland from here, walking across fields and through the former lead and silver mines at Pentireglaze. Our final stretch takes us across fields to the grade I-listed St Enodoc Church at Trebetherick – once known as Sinkininny Church as the surrounding dunes threatened to bury it beneath the sand – before we head back to the sea at Rock.

PENTIRE POINT

DISTANCE: 17.6KM/10.9MILES » **TOTAL ASCENT**: 390M/1,279FT » **START GR**: SW 928757 » **TIME**: ALLOW 5.5 HOURS **SATNAV**: PL27 6LD » **MAP**: OS EXPLORER 106, NEWQUAY & PADSTOW, 1:25,000 » **REFRESHMENTS**: THE MARINERS IN ROCK, OR STEIN'S FISH AND CHIPS IN PADSTOW » **NAVIGATION**: SIMPLE, EITHER ON THE COAST PATH OR INLAND ON LANES AND FOOTPATHS.

DAYMER BAY FROM BREA HILL

10 PENTIRE POINT

Directions – Pentire Point

➎ From the ferry slipway or the nearby car park join the South West Coast Path (SWCP) and follow it north either on the beach or just inland on the dunes. **Stay left** of Brea House but then take a narrow path **right** around the back of the house and up on to the open hillside of Brea Hill. Climb to the top and then descend the steep northern slope to the sand and a small footbridge at the southern end of Daymer Bay.

2 Cross the bridge and follow the coast path through the dunes or walk up the beach to the concrete steps into the car park. **Turn left** here and continue along the coast path around Trebetherick Point and then north-east along the Greenaway Beach to the large sandy beach of Hayle Bay at Polzeath. Cross the beach to some concrete steps on the other side of the bay, or if the tide is high, follow the SWCP waymarkers through Polzeath. Continue north, joining a short section of road that curves around to the right, and then **turn left** down a path to Pentireglaze Haven.

3 Cross this beach and continue on the coast path heading generally north-west out to Pentire Point and all the way around this headland, passing The Rumps and then heading south-eastwards past Com Head and the impressive Lundy Hole. Towards the far end of Lundy Hole, **turn right** on to a footpath heading steeply uphill and then **bearing right** across a couple of fields to some farm buildings at Porteath. Follow the farm track straight ahead to the road by the Bee Centre.

4 **Turn right** on to this road and follow it carefully for a short section before taking the **left** road at the fork on to a smaller road signed to Mesmear Farm. Follow this past the farm for about 1km to a T-junction where you cross the road and join a footpath **straight ahead**, crossing the next field. **Turn left** at the fork on to the track and follow it downhill **ignoring** a track on the left, around a sharp left bend, and in a straight line back uphill next to a golf course. **Turn right** towards the clubhouse but continue past it, following a fence line and then a series of white stones across the golf course. Leave the golf course across a stile and a ditch then cross two fields on a footpath that ends at a road between some houses.

5 Cross the road on to another footpath straight ahead and across two fields, aiming at the small tower of St Enodoc Church. The path passes to the left of the church and then follows white stones across another section of golf course, curving to the left to a small bridge. Cross the bridge and **turn left** on to the track, then almost immediately **turn right** on to a footpath that heads straight to the SWCP just before Brea House. **Turn left** here and return to the start.

ST ENODOC CHURCH FROM BREA HILL

BRIDGE ON TO THE ISLAND FROM BARRAS NOSE

11 Boscastle & Tintagel

14.9km/9.3miles

A walk steeped in historical significance, both recent and ancient, and a classic stretch of the rugged north Cornwall coast.

Boscastle Harbour » Trevalga Cliff » Barras Nose » Tintagel » St Nectan's Glen » Boscastle

Start

Boscastle car park. GR: SX 099912.

The Walk

In August 2004 the village of Boscastle hit the headlines after it experienced one of the most extreme floods ever recorded in Britain. In one afternoon 185 millimetres of rain fell on high ground just inland of the village causing the river to rise by two metres in just an hour. Helicopters rescued 150 people, 75 cars were swept into the sea and 100 homes and businesses were destroyed; incredibly there were no major injuries. Following years of restoration, the village now looks like a quintessentially Cornish place once more, nestled either side of the river at the bottom of a deep, green valley. Beyond, the harbour walls mirror the overlapping headlands that shelter this peaceful inlet from the sea.

From Boscastle our walk follows a stunning stretch of the South West Coast Path (SWCP) with headlands, inlets, outcrops and secret sandy beaches that are well worth taking some time to explore along the way. Our route turns inland at popular Tintagel, the National Trust's first coastal acquisition in 1897, and the coast here and around neighbouring Barras Nose is spectacular. The castle itself, steeped in Arthurian legend, is owned by English Heritage and requires membership or entry fees to explore.

The inland section of our walk winds its way through Tintagel town, passing the wonderful medieval post office, before diving into tranquil St Nectan's Glen. There's a series of stunning waterfalls here (paid entry but visible from the main path) and excellent walking on woodland trails. Climbing up and out of the glen the final stretch of the route traverses open grassland with wonderful views out across the countryside to the coast before descending back into Boscastle to finish.

BOSCASTLE & TINTAGEL

DISTANCE: 14.9KM/9.3MILES » **TOTAL ASCENT**: 808M/2,651FT » **START GR**: SX 099912 » **TIME**: ALLOW 5 HOURS **SATNAV**: PL35 0HE » **MAP**: OS EXPLORER 111, BUDE, BOSCASTLE & TINTAGEL, 1:25,000 » **REFRESHMENTS**: THE NATIONAL TRUST BOSCASTLE CAFE » **NAVIGATION**: SIMPLE, COAST PATH AND INLAND ROADS OR FOOTPATHS.

11 BOSCASTLE & TINTAGEL

Directions – Boscastle & Tintagel

➎ Leave the car park and **turn left**, following the main road towards the sea and crossing the bridge to the south side of the River Valency. **Turn right** on to the minor road which follows the river towards the sea at Boscastle Harbour. After a short distance **turn left** on to the South West Coast Path which heads uphill and then out along the moorland slope to the coast. Stay on the coast path as it curves around to the left and follows the coast in a south-westerly direction, eventually reaching Tintagel Haven, but make sure you take some time to detour out to the various headlands and inlets along the way to admire the views.

2 Just past Tintagel Haven but before the castle, **turn left** off the SWCP, passing the beach cafe before joining Castle Road and following this into Tintagel village. **Bear right** on to Fore Street, passing the National Trust Old Post Office and continuing on to Bossiney Road through the centre of town. Shortly after passing Trenale Lane on your right, **turn right** over a stone stile on to a footpath heading east across three fields and a footbridge to reach another lane.

3 **Turn right** on to the lane and follow it for a short distance before **turning left** on to a footpath between some houses and across two fields to another lane. **Turn left** on to this lane and follow it to a sharp left bend with a gate and stile on the right. **Turn right** here and follow a footpath across a field and then trend right down a hill into some woods.

4 Follow the track contouring downhill to a small footbridge over a stream; cross this and **turn right** on to the path, crossing two more small bridges and then climbing some rocky steps to The Hermitage. Follow the footpath between the buildings and on to the vehicle track behind them. **Turn right** on to the track and follow it north-east along the river. Continue on the track when it bears left away from the river to a path junction at SX 088888. **Keep left** here and trend north-east to reach buildings and a road at Tredole Farm.

5 **Turn left** on to the road and follow it for a short distance to where the road curves to the left. **Turn right** on to a footpath and follow it north across a large field to another lane. **Turn right** on the lane and then **left** on to a footpath just past another left turning. This follows a farm track heading north-east across five fields to join Gibbs Lane near Tubbs Ground Farm. **Turn left** and follow Gibbs Lane then Paradise Road to a T-junction with the B3263 in Boscastle.

6 **Turn right** on to the B3263 (Barnpark Road), then **turn left** down Potters Lane, then **right** down Forrabury Hill to reach the B3263 again, now called New Road. Cross and **turn right** down the no entry Dunn Street, and **turn left** at the bottom of this hill on to Old Road. Follow this downhill to the bridge over the Valency at Boscastle Harbour, recross and **turn right** back to the start.

CAMELOT CASTLE HOTEL FROM BARRAS NOSE

12 Bude to Widemouth Bay

14.7km/9.1miles

A varied route of dramatic coastline, sandy beaches, fascinating geology and a stretch of the historical Bude Canal.

Northcott Mouth » Bude » Compass Point » Salthouse » Helebridge » Bude » Crooklets » Northcott Mouth

Start

National Trust Northcott Mouth car park. GR: SS 203084.

The Walk

Bude is justly famous for its beaches and its geology, both of which are central features of our walk around the far north-east of Cornwall. Bude's rocks are the only ones in the county composed of Carboniferous sandstone, and the folded, stratified cliffs along this stretch of the coast give their name to the internationally recognised 'Bude Formation'. Many of these formations can be seen from the South West Coast Path (SWCP), which scales the clifftops and passes through the town of Bude.

Our walk begins along the coast path, taking in a dramatic stretch along Maer Cliff before descending over the downs to Crooklets Beach, a popular stretch of golden sand edged by rock pools that are also fascinating to explore. From here we follow the SWCP right through Bude before

climbing steeply up to the headland at Compass Point. The Bude Formation at Chapel Rock below is well worth a detour, from where there are also excellent views along the coast in both directions.

A long, spectacular section of the SWCP now brings us to Salthouse, overlooking the vast, sandy beach at Widemouth Bay, popular with families and surfers. Here our walk takes us inland, crossing fields to Helebridge where we join the Bude Canal, built in 1823 to transport mineral-rich sand from the coast to fertilise the fields. Through its 35-mile length it only had two locks – in the section nearest the sea at Bude – with the remaining height difference managed by hauling wheeled tub boats up inclined planes. Pleasant waterside walking brings us back into Bude to return to the start.

BUDE TO WIDEMOUTH BAY

DISTANCE: 14.7KM/9.1MILES » **TOTAL ASCENT**: 366M/1,201FT » **START GR**: SS 203084 » **TIME**: ALLOW 3.5 HOURS **SATNAV**: EX23 9ED » **MAP**: OS EXPLORER 111, BUDE, BOSCASTLE & TINTAGEL AND OS EXPLORER 126, CLOVELLY & HARTLAND, 1:25,000 » **REFRESHMENTS**: THE BUSH INN, MORWENSTOW » **NAVIGATION**: EASY COAST PATH OR CANAL PATH WITH SHORT SECTIONS OF FOOTPATH JOINING THEM.

Directions – Bude to Widemouth Bay

S→ From the car park follow the road down towards the sea. **Turn left** on to the South West Coast Path heading south along the clifftops until you reach a road above Crooklets Beach. **Stay right** on the coast path, following the waymarkers slightly inland into Bude. **Turn right** and cross the river via a bridge and then **keep right**, staying on the coast path until you reach the canal. **Turn right** following the canal towards the sea and cross at the footbridge by the lock gates.

2 **Turn right** and continue on the SWCP past the boathouse and in front of some houses and then along a narrow path towards the breakwater. (It's worth dropping down – with care – to the beach here to see the Bude Formation, formed some 300 million years ago.) Follow the coast path uphill to the tower on Compass Point, onwards over Efford Beacon and eventually running parallel to the road at Upton. Continue south, staying on the coast path that runs between the cliff and the road, venturing out to the various promontories along this stretch of coast should you wish. Finally reach a path junction at Salthouse just before the vast, sandy expanse of Widemouth Bay.

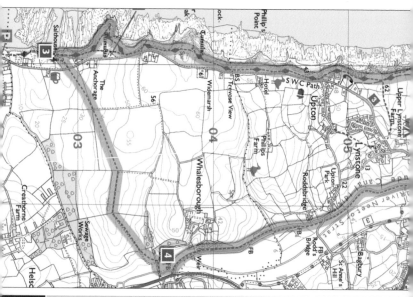

3 Turn **sharp left** on to a track that crosses the road just north/to the left of the Bay View Inn and follow a footpath generally north-eastwards across five fields to a track. **Turn right** and then **left** into a parking area near the Weir Bistro. Take the **right-hand track** at the end of the car park before you cross the river on the right via a footbridge.

4 **Turn left** on to the riverside path and follow it, joining the canal path after a weir. Follow the Bude Canal all the way into Bude. Leave the canal when you reach the main road bridge, **turning right** and crossing the road, walking a short distance before **turning left** on to Ergue-Gaberic Way. Follow this round to the right, rejoining the SWCP and retracing the outbound route over the footbridge and turning **left** to walk back to Crooklets Beach.

5 **Turn right** here, leaving the outbound path and heading up a road named Crooklets. At the top of the hill, **bear left** to cut through between houses on to a small path to Maer Down Road. **Turn left** here and follow the bridleway north across fields to the start.

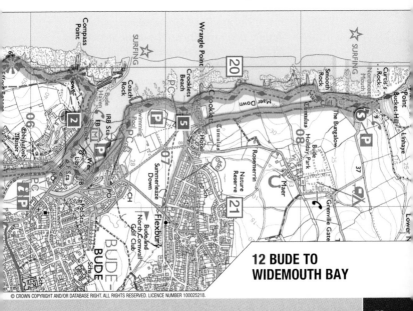

12 BUDE TO WIDEMOUTH BAY

SECTION 4

The South Coast

Just across the Tamar from the busy city of Plymouth, the chapel-topped promontory of Rame Head lies at the southernmost tip of the Rame Peninsula. An adventure even to reach, the headland feels removed and wild despite its proximity to Plymouth Sound. Heading west past the pretty fishing villages of Looe and Polperro, the natural harbour of the Fowey estuary and its network of wooded creeks is a delight to explore. This undulating section of the coast path has hundreds of steps cut into the steep hillsides: challenging for the legs but well worth it for the views from the tops.

Across Carrick Roads from Falmouth, the Roseland Peninsula is a fascinating place with a character all of its own. Green, peaceful and relatively untouched by mass tourism this is a great place to explore on foot, taking in the area's rich history and wildlife.

LANTIC BAY (ROUTE 15)

ST MAWES FROM CARRICKNATH POINT

13 Around Roseland

15.1km/9.4miles

A walk around the tip of the Roseland Peninsula with its interesting military history, wooded creek and dramatic coastline.

St Anthony Head » Porthmellin Head » Towan Beach » Portscatho » Porth Farm » St Anthony Church » Lighthouse » St Anthony Head

Start

St Anthony Head National Trust car park. GR: SW 848313.

The Walk

St Anthony Head overlooks Carrick Roads, one of the world's largest natural harbours. The views from the headland are breathtaking, out across the water to St Mawes, Falmouth and along the coastline in either direction. St Anthony's position as a lookout was utilised by the military in the past and the recently uncovered battery, decommissioned in 1956 and acquired by the National Trust in 1959, is thoroughly interesting to explore. Despite its history, this scenic place is now wonderfully peaceful, and rich in local wildlife from seals to songbirds. Boats chug past below and the blue sea glitters in the sunshine. Should you wish you can stay in the National Trust-owned former officers' quarters right on the headland and take in the harbour views both night and day.

Our walk begins by the holiday cottages and follows the South West Coast Path (SWCP) through clifftop fields before descending to Towan Beach, a great place to explore at any time of the year, dog friendly and with a vintage tea van called Earl providing refreshments over the warmer months. From Towan Beach we continue along the coast path to Portscatho, overlooking Gerrans Bay in a sheltered spot that makes it popular with swimmers. There's a shop and pub here should you be looking for half-time refreshments.

From Portscatho we head inland, walking parallel to the coast along surfaced lanes, paths and a well-made track with the sea stretching out to the left and a pretty, wooded valley to the right. At Porth Farm we follow the banks of Porth Creek through peaceful woodland with glimpses now and again out to the Percuil River. An intriguing section through a churchyard brings us back to the coast path where great views accompany us all the way back to the start.

AROUND ROSELAND

DISTANCE: 15.1KM/9.4MILES » **TOTAL ASCENT**: 546M/1,791FT » **START GR**: SW 848313 » **TIME**: ALLOW 5 HOURS **SATNAV**: TR2 5HA » **MAP**: OS EXPLORER 105, FALMOUTH & MEVAGISSEY, 1:25,000 » **REFRESHMENTS**: 'EARL', THE THIRSTEA COMPANY'S VINTAGE CITROËN VAN, IS PARKED AT PORTH FARM SEASONALLY FROM EASTER TO NOVEMBER » **NAVIGATION**: SIMPLE COAST PATH AND A SHORT SECTION OF INLAND TRACK.

13 AROUND ROSELAND

Directions – Around Roseland

➤ Leave the car park heading south-west past the holiday cottages – formerly officers' quarters – to the old battery on St Anthony Head. **Turn left** behind the gun emplacements and follow the South West Coast Path around Zone Point and then north-east along the edge of a series of fields joined by stiles above the cliffs. Follow the path down to Towan Beach looking out for seals on the rocks around Killigerran Head.

> **SC:** You can **turn left** at Towan Beach and cut across to rejoin and shorten the route at Porth Farm (point 3), making a 9km (5.6 miles) loop.

2 Continue north on the SWCP past Greeb Point and Raven's Hole to join a road on the edge of Portscatho. **Turn left** on to the road and follow it until you can **turn left** between some houses, leaving the coast path and joining a footpath signed to Percuil. Follow the footpath across a field and beside a campsite to reach Treloan Lane. **Turn left** on to the lane and follow it to its end where it turns into a surfaced bridleway. Continue on the bridleway for about 2km to the road at Porth Farm.

3 **Turn sharp right** on to the road and follow it for a short stretch until you can **turn left** and cross a footbridge into a field. **Turn right** and follow the footpath along the bank of Porth Creek and through the woodland, around North-hill Point and south-west to rejoin the SWCP at the edge of Cellars Beach where you will shortly reach the road in St Anthony. Follow the road for a short section passing Place House, then **turn right** down a track to the church.

4 Follow the path through the churchyard and out on to a track which follows the edge of the cove around Cellars Beach. **Fork left** staying on the SWCP before the track starts curving to the right, and follow the path uphill over a field and down to the coast of St Mawes Harbour. **Turn left** and continue following the coast path around Carricknath Point and south to a small beach and a footbridge.

5 Cross the bridge and stay right on the SWCP past the old paraffin store to the lighthouse. Take the **sharp left turn** and head uphill back to the start.

VAULT BEACH

14 Dodman Point & Portmellon

14.7km/9.1miles

A walk around south Cornwall's highest headland through fishing villages, beaches and a rich literary and archaeological past.

Penare » Hemmick Beach » Dodman Point » Gorran Haven » Chapel Point » Portmellon » Gorran Churchtown » Penare

Start

Penare National Trust car park.
GR: SW 999404.

The Walk

Our walk begins in the peaceful hamlet of Penare, heading straight for the sea and the South West Coast Path (SWCP). Shortly after joining the coast path we pass the Bulwark, a huge Iron Age earthwork some 600 metres long and six metres high in places that would have served as a fortification. From here we continue to the granite cross and fine views at Dodman Point, the highest headland on the south coast of Cornwall at 114 metres. The cross was erected in 1896 as a navigational aid for seafarers. Continuing along the coast we reach Vault Beach, a wide sand and shingle curve that's well worth a detour to explore, before rounding the headland at Maenease Point and descending to Gorran Haven, a traditional Cornish fishing village in a sheltered cove between two sandy beaches.

The next main beach along the coast is Great Perhaver, sheltered and a good swimming spot, although a bit of a scramble to reach; our route continues around the headland at Chapel Point, which features in Daphne du Maurier's *The House on the Strand*. The beach here, nestling between Chapel Point and Turbot Point, is Colona Beach, edged by rocky spits and inaccessible by car, making it a perfect alternative to the busier beaches nearby. Just inland from here is Bodrugan's Leap, named after Sir Henry Bodrugan who, charged with treason in 1487, made a tremendous leap over the cliffs into a waiting boat to escape the army of Sir Richard Edgcumbe.

A little further along we come to Portmellon, a pleasant settlement with a sandy beach at low tide. Here we turn inland for our return trip to Penare, taking in a wonderful variety of open coastal grassland, river valleys and peaceful woodland.

DODMAN POINT & PORTMELLON

DISTANCE: 14.7KM/9.1MILES » **TOTAL ASCENT**: 691M/2,267FT » **START GR**: SW 999404 » **TIME**: ALLOW 5 HOURS **SATNAV**: PL26 6NY » **MAP**: OS EXPLORER 105, FALMOUTH & MEVAGISSEY, 1:25,000 » **REFRESHMENTS**: THE BARLEY SHEAF, GORRAN » **NAVIGATION**: SIMPLE COAST PATH AND INLAND LANES OR PATHS.

14 DODMAN POINT & PORTMELLON

Directions – Dodman Point & Portmellon

⊙→ Leave the car park and cross the road, **turning right** and climbing a couple of steps on to a footpath signed *Hemmick Beach ¼ mile*. The footpath heads north-west initially before following the road to the coast. **Turn left** on to the South West Coast Path and follow it south along the cliff edge to Dodman Point. Continue on the coast path around the headland and then north with the sea on your right passing Bow or Vault Beach and Pen-a-maen or Maenease Point to eventually reach the road in Gorran Haven.

2 Stay on the coast path, following waymarkers through Gorran Haven village along Church Street, **turning right** on to Cliff Road and following this to its end at the northern edge of the village. Join the path at the end of the road and continue above the cliffs in a north-easterly direction to Turbot Point. From here the SWCP trends north-west for about 1.5km, joining a track and then a road into Portmellon. **Turn right** on to the larger road for a short section to reach Portmellon Cove.

3 **Turn left** off the road, leaving the SWCP and heading through a boatyard to the left of a small stream. Follow this lane inland then join a footpath heading west along the edge of four fields. Cross a path junction with a footbridge to your right but continue on your path as it curves to the left, crossing a stream and passing through some woodland descending steeply. Cross three more fields to join a driveway at some houses. **Turn left** on to this and follow it south to Gorran Churchtown.

4 **Turn right** on to the road passing the church on your right. **Turn left** on to the main road through the village heading south-east. At the T-junction on the edge of the village a footpath on the right of the road leaves the road but follows its course – much more pleasant and safer than walking on the road. The path emerges from this junction; cross the minor road here and follow a footpath sign south through Menagwins Farm and then out and across four fields to a road by another farm.

5 **Turn left** on to the road and follow it until you reach a **sharp right turn** at a road junction. Follow the minor road straight ahead towards Treveague Farm. **Turn right** in the farmyard and follow the footpath past the camping fields to reach a crossroads. Cross straight over and continue downhill and through Penare until you return to the car park and the start.

15 **Lansallos & Polruan**

16.9km/10.5miles

An enjoyable rollercoaster ride of a walk with dramatic headlands, pretty villages, creeks, coves and excellent beaches.

Pencarrow car park » Lantic Bay » Polruan » Churchtown Farm » Triggabrowne » Lansallos » Pencarrow Head » Pencarrow car park

Start

**National Trust Pencarrow car park
GR: SX 149513.**

The Walk

This undulating section of the South West Coast Path (SWCP) is sometimes likened to a rollercoaster and, when you're walking here, it's easy to see why. None of the hills goes on for too long, but the rolling land alternates with enjoyable regularity between wave-washed sea level and high headlands where the views are definitely worth the climb.

Our walk begins by heading straight out on to the coast path and traversing above Lantic Bay, a wide scoop of sand that has a wonderful feeling of wildness about it, backed by high cliffs. We soon descend steeply into the small fishing village and sheltered harbour at Polruan with its tiny winding streets and 14th-century block-house tower (once one of a pair) that stands guard over the entrance to the River Fowey.

Our route now takes us along the steep-sided and densely-wooded banks of the tidal creek at Pont Pill, emerging on to a tiny, tree-lined lane to reach Churchtown Farm before following a footpath up the steep hill to reach higher ground at Pencarrow, where we began our walk several miles earlier. The walk's eastern loop heads through Triggabrowne to the village of Lansallos. There's not much here other than a church but it's a beautiful and peaceful place and Lansallos Cove feels hidden and adventurous. The track that follows a pretty stream down West Combe (not part of this walk but an enjoyable addition or shortcut) was heavily used in the past, possibly for smuggling. From Lansallos a pleasant loop along a mixture of quiet lanes and footpaths brings us back on to the clifftops for the final stretch along the SWCP accompanied by glorious views and a few more of those leg-sapping hills.

LANSALLOS & POLRUAN

DISTANCE: 16.9KM/10.5MILES » **TOTAL ASCENT**: 703M/2,306FT » **START GR**: SX 149513 » **TIME**: ALLOW 5.5 HOURS
SATNAV: PL23 1NP » **MAP**: OS EXPLORER 107, ST AUSTELL & LISKEARD, 1:25,000 » **REFRESHMENTS**: THE LUGGER INN,
POLRUAN » **NAVIGATION**: EASY, MOSTLY SIGNED COAST PATH OR COUNTRY LANES.

Directions — Lansallos & Polruan

➡ **Turn left** out of the car park and cross the larger lane. Go through the gate and **turn right** to follow the footpath parallel to the road. **Turn left** after the next gate following the path along the hedge towards the sea and joining the signposted South West Coast Path at a gate. **Turn right** to follow the SWCP west above Lantic Bay to Polruan.

2 Stay on the SWCP, following waymarkers along the winding lanes down into Polruan and around the headland in the village. Pass The Lugger Inn and then leave the SWCP (which takes the ferry over to Fowey) and continue on a lane that turns into a footpath through some woodland along the bank of Pont Pill creek. The path follows the creek through the woods until you reach a lane. **Turn left** on to this and follow it downhill to a stream and a sharp left-hand bend by Little Churchtown Farm.

3 Leave the road at the bend and **turn right** on to a footpath heading up the valley, past St Wyllow Church, until you reach a road. **Turn left** on to the road and follow it back to the start point.

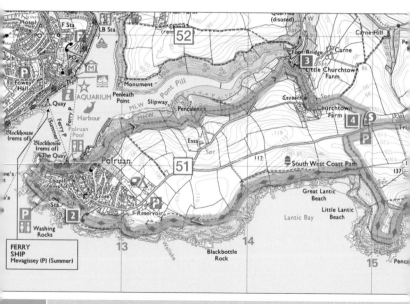

4 To begin the eastern loop of the walk, **turn left** at the junction of the main road past the car park and follow this road downhill past Triggabrowne, taking the **right–hand fork** at the next junction. Follow this smaller road uphill for 1km, then **turn right** on to a footpath at a sharp left turn in the road.

5 Follow the footpath downhill, across a stream and then uphill across two fields to emerge into the village of Lansallos by the church. **Turn right** on to the road here and follow it uphill through the village for 1km to the road junction in Windsor at the top of the hill. **Turn right** here and continue along the lane for 500m, staying **right** where the road forks, to reach a footpath with a gate and stile on the right. **Turn right** here and follow the track generally south-west along the edges of four fields to reach the coast.

6 **Turn right** on to the SWCP and follow it west along Lansallos Cliff to the sandy beach at West Combe. Continue on the coast path around Pencarrow Head and then back to the gate junction above Lantic Bay. Rejoining the outward route, leave the coast path and go through the gate continuing **straight ahead** and follow the path inland along the edge of the field, **turning right** through the gate and back to the start.

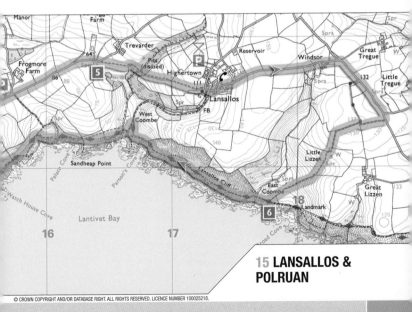

15 LANSALLOS & POLRUAN

16 Rame Head

19.5km/12.1miles

A walk around Cornwall's forgotten corner taking in a medieval chapel, a country estate and glorious coastal scenery.

Cawsand » Wiggle » Rame Head » Penlee Point » Cawsand » Kingsand » Picklecombe Point » Wilderness Point » Mount Edgcumbe » Maker Farm » Kingsand » Cawsand

Start

Cawsand car park. GR: SX 431502.

The Walk

Tucked into the south-easternmost part of the county, just across The Sound from Plymouth, the Rame Peninsula is sometimes described as Cornwall's forgotten corner. But there's a great variety of landscapes and points of interest to be found here, from the rocky shoreline punctuated with popular sandy beaches and the distinctive rounded landmark of Rame Head, crowned with its medieval chapel, to the formal gardens at Mount Edgcumbe Country Park. The valley behind Rame Head shelters the twin villages of Cawsand and Kingsand, while further afield sparse settlements are linked by a network of winding lanes and footpaths.

Our walk begins in the upper reaches of Cawsand, once renowned for being a smuggling village and home to no less than three pubs. From here we climb up and over the headland to reach the South West Coast Path (SWCP) above Whitsand Bay, a three-mile stretch of sand between Rame Head and Portwrinkle. Heading south brings us to Rame Head itself, the site of an Iron Age promontory fort, then a Celtic hermitage, and on which now stands the empty shell of a 14th-century chapel. It's worth taking a moment here to explore the chapel and take in the incredible views.

Descending from Rame Head we continue on the coast path around Penlee Point, through Cawsand and into neighbouring Kingsand, part of Devon until the border was moved in 1844. Rounding Wilderness Point brings us to Mount Edgcumbe Country Park with its grade I listed gardens and grade II listed house. The final stretch of our walk takes us inland along part of Sustrans' National Cycle Network (NCN), finishing through Kingsand and Cawsand.

RAME HEAD

DISTANCE: 19.5KM/12.1MILES » TOTAL ASCENT: 826M/2,710FT » START GR: SX 431502 » TIME: ALLOW 6.5 HOURS
SATNAV: PL10 1PA » MAP: OS EXPLORER 108, LOWER TAMAR VALLEY & PLYMOUTH, 1:25,000 » REFRESHMENTS: THE CAREW ARMS, ANTONY » NAVIGATION: EASY, MOSTLY COAST PATH WITH SOME INLAND FOOTPATHS AND LANES.

RAME HEAD

16 RAME HEAD

Directions – Rame Head

⑤ Leave the car park and **turn right** on to the road, following it slightly uphill to a signed footpath on the **left**. Take this and follow it westwards on to the hillside and across a field to a lane. Go through the gate and cross the lane following a footpath, initially along a driveway into Wringford Farm. Follow this track past the right of the buildings and out across another couple of fields – the track trending left when you begin to approach another lane at Wiggle.

2 **Turn left** on to the lane and follow it downhill to a parking area in a triangular island in the road. **Turn right** here and then cross the next road to reach the coast above Wiggle Cliff. **Turn left** on to the signed South West Coast Path and follow it south-east for about 2km to the old chapel on Rame Head.

3 Continue on the coast path, initially heading north-east and then following the coast east to Penlee Point. Carry on north up the coast, joining a section of road through the villages of Cawsand and Kingsand and then back on to a footpath, either the low footpath or higher SWCP along Minadew Brakes. Reach another road inland from Hooe Lake Point.

4 **Turn right** on to the road and follow it, then after a short distance follow the coast path off to the **left** through a gate into Mount Edgcumbe Country Park. Continue following SWCP waymarkers as the path runs parallel to the road through woodland and around Fort Picklecombe. The path ventures closer to the coast around Redding Point and trends north above cliffs on improving paths, passing a fort, and on until you reach the formal gardens, the garden battery and then the orangery at Wilderness Point. Follow the path around the headland, then leaving the formal gardens, **turn left** on to National Cycle Network Route 2.

5 Head south on The Avenue, passing the Ice House and keeping to the right of Mount Edgcumbe house. Follow a short section of road to the Drywalk car park and then **turn left** at a fork, still following NCN Route 2 to Maker Church. **Turn left** just after the church and leave the cycleway, **turning right** almost straight away, following a footpath south-west across fields to a road near Maker Farm.

6 **Turn right** on to the road and then **right** at the next junction. **Turn left** on to a footpath just before the sharp bend in the road. Follow the footpath south across a field and back to the road. **Turn right** on to the road and then after a few metres **turn left** on to another signed footpath heading downhill towards the sea. Follow this path as it turns right and traverses above the Minadew Brakes and joins a road into Kingsand. Follow Garrett Street through Kingsand and down to Cawsand. **Turn right** on to St Andrew's Street and follow this uphill back to the start.

WHITSAND BAY

SECTION 5

Bodmin & the Tamar Valley

Bodmin Moor is Cornwall's only extensive upland area, an open landscape dominated by granite outcrops and high, rocky tors. It is home to Cornwall's two highest peaks, Rough Tor, 400 metres, and the slightly taller Brown Willy, at 420 metres. Water from the heather-clad bog and marshland on the high moors drains into deep river valleys wooded with ancient oaks, making for varied and interesting walks. The area has a rich cultural heritage, with more than a hundred Bronze Age hut circles excavated on the slopes of Rough Tor, along with a Neolithic enclosure and the foundations of a medieval chapel.

To the east of Bodmin Moor the Tamar Valley takes in an extraordinary variety of landscapes and views, including the much-photographed Calstock Viaduct, while to the west lie the towns of Bodmin and Lostwithiel and the tranquil Lanhydrock Estate.

HELMAN TOR

17 Lanhydrock

18.2km/11.3miles

A varied and enjoyable circuit taking in the magnificent Lanhydrock estate and the Helman Tor National Nature Reserve.

Lostwithiel » Restormel » Newton » Lanhydrock House » Red Moor » Helman Tor » Lanlivery » Lostwithiel

Start

Lostwithiel Community Centre, close to the railway station. GR: SX 105599. Alternative: National Trust car park at Lanhydrock (SX 084637, PL30 5AD).

The Walk

The town of Lostwithiel sits nestled in a wooded valley at the tidal reach of the River Fowey. Home to a train station and plenty of shops, cafes and pubs it's a perfect place to begin our walk. From Lostwithiel we follow the Fowey upstream to Restormel Castle. Overlooking the river, the castle was originally constructed by the Normans, but the current circular keep was built in the 13th century. It is open to the public and well worth a visit for its intriguing history and fine views.

Continuing upstream we reach the National Trust's Lanhydrock estate, with its magnificent grade I listed Victorian house and 890 acres of surrounding land. Much of the estate itself is free to access, although the house and gardens require payment or membership of the trust to enter. Our route follows woodland and riverside trails through the estate before emerging on to open moorland at the foot of Helman Tor. Here we follow a waymarked Wildlife Trust Wilderness Trail, part of a 500-acre wetland and National Nature Reserve, to join the Saints' Way, a 27-mile route right across Cornwall from Padstow on the north coast to Fowey on the south coast. Keep a look out for rare marsh fritillary butterflies in this area in early summer. A brief out-and-back detour takes us to the summit of Helman Tor, a Scheduled Ancient Monument with a logan (rocking) stone, prehistoric hill fort and stone hut circles. The final section of our walk follows the Saints' Way along a fine, grassy ridge and down through the village of Lanlivery and back towards the River Fowey and Lostwithiel.

LANHYDROCK

DISTANCE: 18.2KM/11.3MILES » **TOTAL ASCENT**: 458M/1,503FT » **START GR**: SX 105599 » **TIME**: ALLOW 5.5 HOURS **SATNAV**: PL22 0HE » **MAP**: OS EXPLORER 107, ST AUSTELL & LISKEARD, 1:25,000 » **REFRESHMENTS**: NATIONAL TRUST PARK CAFE AT LANHYDROCK » **NAVIGATION**: SIMPLE FOOTPATHS AND LANES.

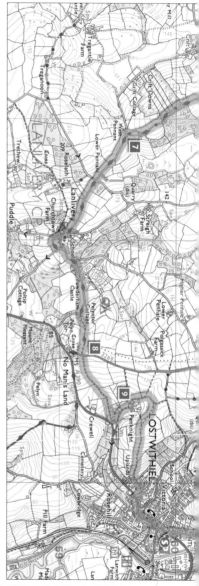

17 LANHYDROCK

Directions – Lanhydrock

⑨ Head north-west to the A390, crossing carefully and following Restormel Road north, signed to the castle. To avoid a section of road, **turn left** after about 1km, going through a gate and **turning right** on to a permissive path running parallel to the road through some Duchy of Cornwall-owned woodland. Continue until you can **turn right** through a gate, back on to the road. **Turn left** here and follow the road to Restormel Farm.

2 Go through the gate and follow footpath signs along a road to the right of the farm buildings and past some cottages. Follow the road as it curves left and heads north-west following the course of the River Fowey for about 2km. Join the track at the water treatment site and cross a couple of fields to a red gate into the Lanhydrock estate.

3 **Turn right** and follow the path, ignoring a fork to the right, and along the river, curving left to a road junction. **Turn right** here and continue until the large gates. **Turn left** through these and head uphill to Lanhydrock House. **Turn left** in front of the house and follow the path through a red gate into the woodland, ignoring a path to the left.

4 Follow the main trail uphill initially heading south-east and then bearing south. Carry on past Garden Cottage and alongside a field before entering woodland again. Continue on the main track downhill ignoring paths to the left and right, cross a bridge and then head uphill to the B3268.

5 **Turn left** on the road and cross carefully, joining a signed footpath almost opposite, through woodland to a road. **Turn right** on to the road and follow it west, **forking left** at the junction and then **turning right** on to the Wildlife Trust Wilderness Trail. Follow this signed trail through woodland, passing a couple of lakes and crossing several sections of boardwalk to reach moorland below Helman Tor. Follow the Wilderness Trail through a gate in the corner of a field and right uphill to join the Saints' Way.

6 **Turn right** on to this path and then **right** again after 500m through a small car park and up an obvious path to the summit of Helman Tor. Enjoy the views and then retrace your steps along the Saints' Way and continue on heading south-east until you reach a road at West Pennant.

7 **Turn left** on to the road, still on the Saints' Way, and straight across the next junction and into Lanlivery. **Fork right** past the church, **stay left** at the next two junctions and **right** at the third, passing right of the entrance to a campsite. **Turn left** on to a footpath after a sharp right bend and cross the following field uphill to a gate in the far left corner. Follow the footpath across the next field to the B3269.

8 Carefully cross straight over and follow the signed footpath to a gate at the bottom left of the large field. Follow the path down to a gate at the bottom right of the next field and then around the bottom of the following field to reach a lane by a house in the far left corner. **Turn left** on to the lane heading uphill to Penknight Farm.

9 Follow the path to the left of the farmhouse to join a footpath between fields. Follow this trending right around the field to a gate into a large field. **Trend right** to a gate into the next field, then **trend left** and follow the path along the hedge line downhill towards Lostwithiel. **Go left** through a gate in the second field and **then right** through a gate with a footpath sign, follow the right-hand hedge line down to a stile and join the footpath downhill to a road. Follow the road curving right downhill to the A390, **turn left** and follow this back to the start.

HELMAN TOR

ROUGH TOR

18 Rough Tor & Brown Willy

16.3km/10.1miles

A walk around the remote reaches of Bodmin Moor taking in Cornwall's highest point and the area's fascinating history.

Rough Tor car park » Stannon Stone Circle » Rough Tor » Brown Willy » Source of the Fowey » Roughtor Plantation » Rough Tor car park

Start

Rough Tor car park. GR: SX 138818.

The Walk

Bodmin Moor covers 208 square kilometres (129 square miles) of granite upland in the east of Cornwall, an open landscape dotted with rocky tors. Particularly over the wetter months there are large areas of marshland making parts of the moor difficult to cross, however there is plenty of excellent walking here, far from the crowds that flock to the coasts, and even in the height of summer few venture into the wilder reaches of Bodmin.

Our walk begins at Poldue Downs and heads straight out on to open moorland and over the gentle rise of Louden Hill to reach Stannon, a place much scarred by china clay works yet still peaceful and remote with its impressive 40-metre stone circle, dating to the late Neolithic or early Bronze Age. From here we climb steeply up to the summit of Rough Tor ('rough' is pronounced 'row',

to rhyme with 'cow') at a high point of 400 metres, from where there are great views on a clear day of the surrounding moorland, the countryside and ocean beyond, and across to our next summits, Little Rough Tor, Showery Tor and Brown Willy.

The summit of Brown Willy is Cornwall's highest point, standing at 420 metres above sea level. Set amid rocky cairns that date back to the early Bronze Age, its unusual name comes from the Cornish 'Bronn Wennili', meaning 'Hill of Swallows'. This place has been considered sacred for thousands of years and the summit cairn is thought by some to be the resting place of an ancient Cornish king. From Brown Willy we cross High Moor, passing the source of the River Fowey and descending from the open moor to finish through the tree-lined trails of Roughtor Plantation and Lower Moor Plantation.

ROUGH TOR & BROWN WILLY

DISTANCE: 16.3KM/10.1MILES » **TOTAL ASCENT**: 467M/1,532FT » **START GR**: SX 138818 » **TIME**: 4.5–5 HOURS » **SATNAV**: PL32 9QG » **MAP**: OS EXPLORER 109, BODMIN MOOR, 1:25,000 » **REFRESHMENTS**: THE OLD INN, ST BREWARD » **NAVIGATION**: FAIRLY OBVIOUS IN GOOD WEATHER BUT SOME SECTIONS OF TRACKLESS OPEN MOOR, SO CONFIDENT NAVIGATION IS NEEDED PARTICULARLY IN POOR VISIBILITY. RETURNING OVER ROUGH TOR FROM BROWN WILLY AVOIDS THE HARDEST NAVIGATION.

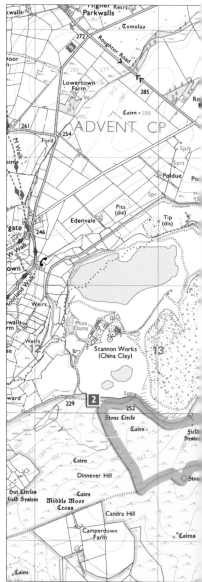

Resr
299

er Moor

Oldpark

Roughtor Mine
(disused)

Lower Moor
Plantation

Lanlavery Rock

BS

Roughtor
Plantation

5

82

P

S

Monument

Cairn

Roughtor
Marsh

Settlement

Tumulus

Cairn

Showery
Tor

Long House

Cairns

Little Rough
Tor

3

Log
Rock

Settlement

Rough Tor

Memorial

Hut Circle

Maiden Tor

Cairns

Source
River Fo

High Moor

14

Roughtor Moors

15

Sprs

16

an Rock

Long House

Hut Circles

Settlement & Field System

Settlement

Field
System

Slades

Fowey
Well

Stone
Circle

Settlement

Hut
Circles

420 Cairn

Brown
Willy

4

House
Platform

Cairn

teping Hill
254

Cairns

Hut Circles

Settlement

Cairn

Village
(site of)

Hut
Circles

Brownwilly

Cairn

Garrow

18 ROUGH TOR & BROWN WILLY

© CROWN COPYRIGHT AND/OR DATABASE RIGHT. ALL RIGHTS RESERVED. LICENCE NUMBER 100025218.

Directions – Rough Tor & Brown Willy

⑤ Head downhill out of the car park and through two gates on to the open moor, cross the river and then **trend right** heading south through a series of ancient hut circles and settlements, slowly gaining height. Roughly follow the edge of the old quarried area around to the right and over Louden Hill. Continue and **bear right** around to the stone circle at the southern end of Stannon china clay works.

2 From the stone circle head south-east and slightly uphill to reach a track. **Turn left** on to this and head east, deviating off the track to visit the other stone circles. After nearly 2km, cross a stream and reach a field system on the right. At the far edge of this, **turn left** off the track and head north past another stone circle across Roughtor Moors and directly up to the summit of Rough Tor.

3 Continue along the ridge over Little Rough Tor and across to Showery Tor to tick off all the tops in the area. Then **turn almost back on yourself** and join the main path heading south downhill to the bridge at the edge of the field systems below Brown Willy. Cross the De Lank River and follow the main path uphill and curving to the right to the trig-pointed summit of Brown Willy.

4 From the summit head downhill in a north-easterly direction past Fowey Well and contouring around in an almost northly direction now on High Moor, using vague paths to find the source of the River Fowey. **Turn left** here and heading in a north-westerly direction contour around the northern end of Roughtor Marsh to the eastern edge of Roughtor Plantation.

5 Follow the southern edge of the plantation and **turn right** on to the forest road into the wood. Follow the track all the way through the wood, trending around to the left through Lower Moor Plantation and back to the car park.

GOLITHA FALLS

19 Golitha Falls & Siblyback Lake   18.1km/11.2miles

A tour of the rivers, lakes and waterfalls that run through the moors and valleys south of Bodmin Moor.

Draynes Bridge Golitha Falls car park » Golitha Falls » Draynes Bridge » Siblyback Lake » Trekeivesteps » Lamelgate Farm » Wortha » Lower Bowden » Lower Trenant » Draynes Bridge car park

Start
Draynes Bridge Golitha Falls car park.
GR: SX 227689.

The Walk
Our walk begins at Golitha Falls, and an exploration of this picturesque valley where the River Fowey flows in a series of cascades and falls through leafy woodland is highly recommended as a way to start or finish. From Golitha we head over Draynes Bridge, built in 1876, and up on to open ground, contouring the hillside below Bulland Downs. From here, footpaths lead off to King Doniert's Stone, two large, engraved blocks from the ninth-century cross that once marked this point. An underground chamber also lies beneath the stones.

Continuing onwards, we take in a pleasant three-mile loop around Siblyback Lake, a reservoir built in the 1960s to meet increasing local water demands. The lake is a popular venue for water sports, including sailing and water skiing, and there's also a cafe and bird hide. The surfaced trail all the way around its perimeter makes for an enjoyable walk, run or cycle at any time of the year, with great views out to Bodmin Moor. On returning to the dam after our circumnavigation of the lake, we follow the River Fowey upstream for a short distance before heading westwards out across open countryside and moorland to Berry Down, with its Iron Age hill fort and trig point summit. Here we join the Two Valleys Walk, a five-mile circular route between the Loveny and Fowey valleys, and follow this through peaceful woodland at Bowden Wood and Periock Wood – a wonderfully shady trail on a warm summer's day. The final section of our walk takes us along quiet country lanes through Draynes and back to the River Fowey and Golitha Falls.

GOLITHA FALLS & SIBLYBACK LAKE
DISTANCE: 18.1KM/11.2MILES » TOTAL ASCENT: 480M/1,575FT » START GR: SX 227689 » TIME: ALLOW 5.5 HOURS
SATNAV: PL14 6RX » MAP: OS EXPLORER 109, BODMIN MOOR, 1:25,000 » REFRESHMENTS: INKIE'S SMOKEHOUSE BBQ, AT DRAYNES BRIDGE CAR PARK » NAVIGATION: SIMPLE FOOTPATHS AND LANES BUT SOME CAN GET A BIT OVERGROWN.

19 GOLITHA FALLS & SIBLYBACK LAKE

Directions – Golitha Falls & Siblyback Lake

➋ Leave the car park, cross the road and follow the signed river path down the River Fowey to explore Golitha Falls. Either return on the same path or use the slightly higher path to make a short circular walk. When you return to the road **turn right**, cross Draynes Bridge and **turn left** following the road past a couple of houses. Take the second footpath sign **right**, following fingerposts with yellow arrows east across moorland and then over a stile into a field. Follow the path across the field, curving round to the left, staying just left of the sewage works to reach a road by a farm.

2 **Turn left** on to the road and follow it uphill and around to the right. Take the signed track **left** next to some old barns and follow the path uphill along the edge of fields following an enclosed track into a large field above Siblyback Lake. Cross this field aiming at the dam to reach a small turning circle through a gate.

3 **Turn right** here and follow the lake path all the way around the lake and back to this point. You can reduce the walk's distance by about 6km if you don't circumnavigate the lake. Having walked around the lake and returned over the dam to point 3, **turn right** through a gate and follow the track downhill to the dam's service road, cross this and follow a path through a gate and into woodland trending right to a footbridge.

4 Cross the bridge and follow the path **left** through a gate into a field and cross this to the opposite corner through a gate and uphill on a track to the houses at North Trekeive. Follow the path between the houses on to the driveway which you follow south-west to the road. **Turn left** and follow this downhill to a junction. **Turn right** on to the larger road and cross the bridge following the road and the River Fowey north. After about 1km **turn left** on to the track to Lamelgate Farm.

5 Follow this track uphill then along a sharp left, staying left past the farmhouse and then follow a signed permissive path in the field around the left edge of the farmyard to reach a gate on the **right**. Go through this and then **immediately left** through another gate on to open moorland. Follow the path uphill with the field boundary on the left passing a path on the left and until you reach the top of the hill.

6 **Turn left** here through a metal gate and follow the footpath trending left following the left boundary to a stile into a field. Cross the field to a fingerpost and **turn right** following the signs across the following three large fields ending over a stile in the bottom right corner. Follow this path down to the driveway at Wortha. Follow this **straight ahead** across a small bridge and then trending left uphill to join a road through East Northwood to a junction with a larger road.

7 **Turn left** on to the road and follow it south uphill and then downhill to a footpath sign on the left opposite an open barn. **Turn left** on to this and follow the path downhill through Periock Wood to a road at Lower Trenant. **Turn left** on to the road and follow it uphill through Draynes and then downhill back to the start.

SIBLYBACK LAKE

20 The Hurlers & the Cheesewring
16.3km/10.1miles

A tour of the fascinating granite features on Bodmin, including naturally formed tors, ancient artefacts and modern quarries.

Minions » The Hurlers » Siblyback » Trewortha » Kilmar Tor » Cheesewring » Minions

Start

Hurlers car park, south-west of Minions village. GR: SX 259710.

The Walk

Minions is the highest village in Cornwall, with most of its buildings lying above 300 metres, an oasis within the wilds of Bodmin Moor where you'll find a shop, cafe, post office and pub. The area surrounding the village is rich in historical artefacts, from Bronze Age megaliths to the remains of 19th- and 20th-century quarrying and mining.

Our walk begins at Minions and follows excellent tracks across open moorland, passing the Hurlers – a series of late Neolithic or early Bronze Age stone circles – and the twin standing stones known as The Pipers, all of which which make for an interesting diversion. Dropping down to Siblyback village – near to Siblyback Lake, a reservoir owned by the South West Lakes Trust and visited on route 19 – we skirt woodland at Smallacoombe Plantations along a disused railway line, part of the Liskeard and Caradon

Railway built around 1844 to transport products from the local mines and quarries to Liskeard and then on to Looe for shipping.

Heading back up on to the high moor we pass Trewortha Farm, home to some replica Bronze Age roundhouses used for educational purposes, and cross Twelve Men's Moor, named after an agreement made in 1285 between Prior Henry of nearby Launceston Priory and 12 local men granting them grazing rights on this part of the moor for an annual fee of four silver shillings. Next, we climb to the summit of Kilmar Tor at 396 metres before following the former railway to the foot of Stowe's Hill. At the top is the Cheesewring, a naturally formed tower of balanced granite boulders, although local legend has it that it was built by an angry giant. The adjacent Cheesewring Quarry, which ceased to be worked in the 1980s, supplied the granite for cladding London's Tower Bridge.

THE HURLERS & THE CHEESEWRING

DISTANCE: 16.3KM/10.1MILES » **TOTAL ASCENT**: 383M/1,257FT » **START GR**: SX 259710 » **TIME**: ALLOW 4.5 HOURS
SATNAV: PL14 5LL » **MAP**: OS EXPLORER 109, BODMIN MOOR, 1:25,000 » **REFRESHMENTS**: CHEESEWRING HOTEL, MINIONS
NAVIGATION: MOSTLY TRACK AND FOOTPATH BUT SOME STRETCHES OF OPEN MOORLAND SO CAN BE TRICKY IN POOR VISIBILITY.

20 THE HURLERS & THE CHEESEWRING

Directions – The Hurlers & the Cheesewring

➤ From the Hurlers car park follow the obvious track north-west past The Pipers – a pair of standing stones – to a track junction. Take the **left fork** to a flooded, disused quarry where the track ends. Follow vague footpaths around the quarry and then south-west across moorland to a long stone row.

2 **Turn right** and follow the path north along the stone row past old settlements and field systems to a wall cutting across the path. Cross the wall and **turn left**, following the wall west to a track by a stream and the edge of some arable fields near Siblyback. Cross the stream and follow the track around the edge of the field to a junction at the far corner; **turn right** here and follow the track between fields and back to the open moor.

3 Continue on the track to the east of more standing stones, hut circles and ancient field systems and gradually curve to the left, following the course of the Withey Brook north to the corner of Smallacoombe Plantations. Follow the track – a dismantled railway – **straight ahead** up the east side of the woodland to grid reference SX 235752 then **turn right** on to a path heading east, crossing the brook and following a bridleway. Pass Trewortha Farm and after 1.5km reach the end of a road.

4 **Turn right** before the road and walk south on a path climbing up on to open moorland, curving to the right to the rocky summit and trig point of Kilmar Tor. From here, **turn left** and drop down the south side of the tor to a track. **Turn right** and follow the track as it curves around Langstone Downs – ignoring tracks to the left and right – to a footpath and the end of the road by Wardbrook Farm, Sharptor.

5 **Turn right** here and follow the trail uphill to the rocky summit of the Cheesewring and the top of the quarry. **Turn left** and follow the path around the top of the quarry and **then right** through the quarry to the old dismantled railway line (no tracks) on the south side. Follow this as it heads south-east and then curves right, south, back to Minions village. **Turn right** when you reach the road in the village to return to the start.

DAY WALKS GUIDEBOOKS

Written by local authors, each pocket-sized guidebook features:

- 20 great day-length walks
- Ordnance Survey 1:25,000-scale maps
- easy-to-follow directions
- distance & navigation information
- refreshment stops & local area information
- a detailed appendix

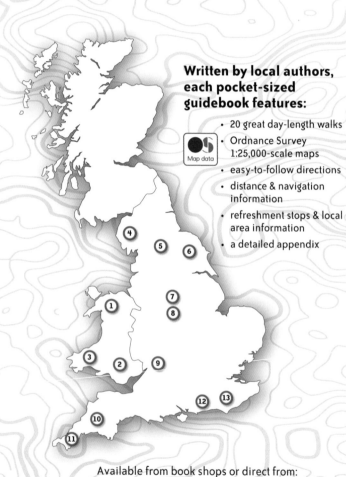

Available from book shops or direct from:

www.v-publishing.co.uk

Appendix

A complete list of good places to eat and stay in Cornwall is beyond the scope of this book – in fact there are books dedicated to the subject – however the following lists represent a small sample that we have tried and tested, or for which we have received reliable recommendations.

Tourist Information

www.visitcornwall.com
Official tourism website for Cornwall.

www.cornwallinfocus.co.uk
Cornwall visitor and tourist information centres.

www.letsgocornwall.com
The official website for Cornwall tourist information centres.

www.visitengland.com/things-to-do/cornwall
The official tourist board for England.

www.visitislesofscilly.com
Official tourism website for Scilly.

Food and Drink
CAFES

Apple Tree Cafe, Land's End	T: 01736 872 753
Porthcurno Beach Cafe, Porthcurno	T: 01736 811 108
Courthouse Cafe, Pendeen	T: 01736 788 662
Kynance Cove Cafe (also cottages)	T: 01326 290 436
Stein's Fish and Chips, Padstow	T: 01841 532 700
Chapel Porth Beach Cafe	T: 01872 552 487
Melinsey Mill, Veryan	T: 01872 501 049
Lansallos Barton Farm, Looe	T: 01503 272 293
Woods Cafe, Cardinham	T: 01208 781 11

PUBS

Fraggle Rock Bar, Bryher, Isles of Scilly	T: 01720 422 222
The Tinners Arms, Zennor	T: 01736 796 927
The Halzephron Inn, Gunwalloe	T: 01326 240 406
The Roseland Inn, Philleigh	T: 01872 580 254
The Blisland Inn	T: 01208 850 739

Accommodation
HOSTELS AND BUNKHOUSES

Old Chapel Backpackers, Zennor	T: 01736 798 307
Beach Head Bunkhouse, Wadebridge	T: 0344 335 1296
Penrose Bunkhouse, Helston	T: 0344 335 1296

YHA youth hostels can be found in the following places, for more information please visit:
www.yha.org.uk

Boscastle	T: 0345 371 9006
Boswinger, St Austell	T: 0345 371 9107
Coverack, Helston	T: 0345 371 9014
Eden Project	T: 0345 371 9573
Land's End	T: 0345 371 9643
Lizard Point	T: 0345 371 9550
Penzance	T: 0345 371 9653
Perranporth	T: 0345 371 9755
Portreath, Redruth	T: 01209 842 244
Tintagel	T: 0345 371 9145
Treyarnon Bay, Padstow	T: 0345 371 9664

HOTELS, B&BS

Mincarlo B&B, St Mary's, Isles of Scilly	T: 01720 422 513
The Old Coastguard Hotel, Mousehole	T: 01736 731 222
The Gurnard's Head, Zennor	T: 01736 796 928

SELF-CATERING

National Trust Holidays	www.nationaltrust.org.uk
Classic Cottages	www.classic.co.uk
The Landmark Trust	www.landmarktrust.org.uk
The Old Stables, Bodmin	www.airbnb.co.uk/rooms/15702626

Camping

Bryher Campsite, Bryher, Isles of Scilly	T: 01720 422 068
Treen Farm Campsite, Treen (no bookings)	T: 07598 469 322

Henry's Campsite, Lizard .... T: 01326 290 596
Teneriffe Farm Campsite, Lizard .... T: 01326 240 293
Highertown Farm Campsite,
Lansallos .... T: 01208 265 211
South Penquite Farm, Blisland .... T: 01208 850 491

Outdoor Shops
Cotswold Outdoor, Truro .... T: 01872 222 032
Mountain Warehouse, St Ives .... T: 01736 793 884

Weather
www.metoffice.gov.uk

Other Publications
Day Walks in Devon
Jen & Sim Benson, Vertebrate Publishing
www.v-publishing.co.uk

Day Walks in the Cotswolds
Judy Mills, Vertebrate Publishing
www.v-publishing.co.uk

Day Walks in the Brecon Beacons
Harri Roberts, Vertebrate Publishing
www.v-publishing.co.uk

South West Mountain Biking
Nick Cotton, Vertebrate Publishing
www.v-publishing.co.uk

PORTHCURNO FROM LOGAN ROCK

About the Authors

Jen and **Sim Benson** are passionate about exploring wild places, whether they're running through the mountains, walking the National Trails or climbing on their local Dartmoor granite. In 2015 they spent a year living under canvas in Britain with their two young children. They are the authors of guidebooks *Day Walks in Devon*, *Wild Running* and *The Adventurer's Guide to Britain*, and the National Trust book *Amazing Family Adventures*, and are regular contributors to a number of outdoor publications including *Outdoor Fitness*, *Trail*, *Country Walking*, *Runner's World* and *Trail Running* magazines and gear experts for *Walk* magazine.

www.jenandsimbenson.co.uk

Vertebrate Publishing

At Vertebrate Publishing we publish books to inspire adventure.

It's our rule that the only books we publish are those that we'd want to read or use ourselves. We endeavour to bring you beautiful books that stand the test of time and that you'll be proud to have on your bookshelf for years to come.

The Peak District was the inspiration behind our first books. Our offices are situated on its doorstep, minutes away from world-class climbing, biking and hillwalking. We're driven by our own passion for the outdoors, for exploration, and for the natural world; it's this passion that we want to share with our readers.

We aim to inspire everyone to get out there. We want to connect readers – young and old – with the outdoors and the positive impact it can have on well-being. We think it's particularly important that young people get outside and explore the natural world, something we support through our publishing programme.

As well as publishing award-winning new books, we're working to make available many out-of-print classics in both print and digital formats. These are stories that we believe are unique and significant; we want to make sure that they continue to be shared and enjoyed.

www.v-publishing.co.uk